Great Chefs of Historic Alexandria

A compilation of delicious recipes from the top
Chefs in Historic Alexandria, Virginia,
celebrating its 250th anniversary.
Accompanied by historical notes and sketches
for a real "taste" of the food and
the ambience of this remarkable "Old Town"..

Bryant Girdler
&
Mimi Winship

Published by Girdler Associates
P.O. Box 525
Boca Raton, Florida 33429

Copyright© 1999

First Printing - - - - - - - - April 1999
Second Printing - - - - - - - July 1999

Library of Congress Catalog Card Number 99-90523

ISBN: 0-9668344-1-0

Printed in the United States of America

In celebrating Alexandria's 250th Anniversary, we honor a diverse and colorful city with strong ties to the past, a vibrant and exciting present and a future full of promise.

And although customs change and the landscape is altered, one thing is always the same, *we love to eat!* So good chefs are always high up on the list of people we admire.

"The Great Chefs of Historic Alexandria" spans our culinary history from Martha Washington to Alexander, the Old Town Mouse, and within its pages you will find recipes from many of our most gifted chefs of today. You will discover who these chefs are and how they came to be here. You'll learn about the restaurants, historic buildings and historic sites so revered by Alexandrians and our visitors and guests.

Think of this as a cook book, a guide book and a history book. Plan your tours around the sites you want to see and the restaurants nearby. Try some of these wonderful recipes yourself. Soak in some local history as you dine.

We would like to thank the City of Alexandria for providing us with a wonderful history, and the Office of Historic Alexandria directed by Jean Federico, the Alexandria Convention and Visitors Association under the leadership of JoAnne Mitchell and the 250th Anniversary Commission headed by Philip Brooks for their assistance and encouragement. And special thanks to Laura Overstreet of the ACVA and the 250th Anniversary Commission and to Pat Gaffney of Union Street Public House for their invaluable suggestions and help.

And, of course, kudos to our chefs, past and present! When you meet these chefs, ask them to sign your book!

Bryant Girdler and Mimi Winship

Great Chefs

of

Historic

Alexandria

Edited and compiled
by
R. Bryant Girdler
and
Mimi Winship

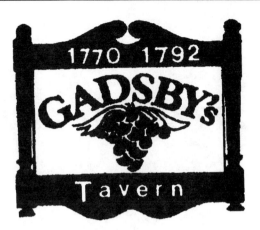

138 North Royal Street
Alexandria, Virginia
(703) 548-1288

Nearly all of the founders of American Independence enjoyed the warm tavern hospitality of Gadsby's Tavern. No public building in America is more intimately associated with the struggle for independence and establishment of national sovereignty. For nearly a century it was a center of political, social and cultural life in this important colonial seaport community. The Tavern, circa 1770, now houses the museum. The City Hotel now houses the restaurant and ballroom. Both were meccas for public figures who established the nation's capital in the City of Washington. The City Hotel was a veritable skyscraper when erected in 1792.

John Gadsby, for whom it is named, gained international renown as the host from 1796 to 1808.

The atmosphere of early America is found today in the famous 18th Century hostelry, which was the setting for brilliant balls for society in the 1700's, meetings of patriots and receptions for several Presidents. In their letters and journals, guests were universal in their praise for the lavishness of life at the Tavern, which was described as the finest public house in America.

George Washington frequently visited these buildings. General & Mrs. Washington attended the annual Birthright Ball held here in his honor, and performed his last military review on the tavern steps.

The buildings are noted for exquisite georgian architecture, preserved & restored to a late 18th century appearance. The restaurant faithfully duplicates the food, serving pieces, furnishings and costumes. The coachyard serves as an adjunct to the indoor dining rooms during the spring, summer and autumn seasons.

The City of Alexandria acquired the buildings from American Legion Post #24 on August 11, 1972. The local veterans organization saved the structure from demolition in 1928. Those who visit Gadsby's Tavern enjoy a truly authentic living experience from the nation's colonial past.

138 North Royal Street • Alexandria, Virginia
(703) 548-1288

Gadsby's Tavern Clam Chowder

1 qt. Milk
2 Cans Chopped Clams
1/4 Lb. diced Onions
3 Celery stalks, diced
8 Tbsp. Butter
1/2 Cup Flour

1/2 Lb. diced red Potatoes
1 oz. Clam Base
1 oz. Sherry
1 oz. Parsley
1/2 oz. Old Bay
1/4 oz. Garlic

Saute onions and Celery in Butter until onions are transparent. Add the Flour to make a "roux". Add the chopped Clams and Milk. Add the already cooked Potatoes. Adjust the thickness and add the remaining ingredients.
Serves 8.

Buttermilk Pye

3 Cups Buttermilk
3 Cups Sugar
4 Tbsp. Flour
1 Tbsp. Lemon Extract

3 Eggs
3/4 Cup melted Margarine
1&1/2 Tsp. Nutmeg
2 Pye Shells (10")

Mix together all ingredients except pie shells.
Blend well and pour into the Pye Shells.
Bake at 350° until firm and golden brown,
about 45 minutes to 1 hour.

Chef Rick Thompson

Gadsby's Tavern
138 North Royal Street
Alexandria, Virginia
(703) 548-1288

A Registered National Historic Landmark

Gadsby's Colonial Pye

2 Cups cooked, chopped Chicken
1 Pkg. Frozen Pastry Dough
1 Cup cooked Salad Shrimp
1/4 Cup diced Celery
1/4 Cup diced Onion
1/4 Cup diced Potato

1 Cup Clam Juice
1/2 gallon Milk
4 oz. Butter
Flour
Old Bay seasoning
Parsley

Melt butter and add flour to make a roux. Add Milk and Clam juice and cook until thickened. Add Chicken, Shrimp and cooked vegetables. Season to taste. Cool and put in individual serving dishes and cover with Pastry dough. Bake in 350° oven until crust is browned and filling is heated through, about 15 minutes. Serves 8-10

Gadsby's Mulled Cider

1 Gallon Apple Cider
20 Cinnamon sticks

2 Tsp. whole Cloves
Piece of string

Place Cinnamon sticks and cloves in a coffee filter. Wrap and tie the filter with the string. Drop in a large pot with the Cider and simmer for 1 hour. Serve alone or with your favorite spirit. We recommend brandy or dark rum.

Chef Rick Thompson

Gadsby's Tavern
138 North Royal Street
Alexandria, Virginia
(703) 548-1288

A Registered National Historic Landmark

Gadsby's Stuffed Pork Loin

5 Lbs. Pork Loin, butterflied
1&1/4 Lbs. Spinach
1&1/4 Lbs. Sausage meat
1 Lb. Onion

1/2 Cup Basil
1 Tbsp. Garlic
1 oz. Sherry
1&1/2 Cups bread crumbs

For the Sauce:
1 Cup Brown Sauce
1&1/2 Tbsp. Dijon Mustard

1 Tbsp. White Wine
1/2 Tbsp. Lemon Juice

Grind Spinach, Sausage and Onion together. Cook
until sausage meat is done.
Add Basil, Garlic and Sherry. Drain.
Add bread crumbs to thicken.
Butterfly the Pork Loin and spread the Spinach
mixture down the center and tie shut to form a log.
Roast in a 350° oven for approximately 1&1/2 hours
in a covered pan.
Combine sauce ingredients, heat and serve with
the Pork Loin. Serves 8

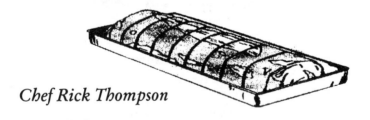

Chef Rick Thompson

Gadsby's Tavern
138 North Royal Street
Alexandria, Virginia
(703) 548-1288

A Registered National Historic Landmark

10

UNION STREET
PUBLIC HOUSE

Originally George Washington surveyed Alexandria. The city plan was then laid out by a civil engineer. Union Street was laid in 1782. Initially the street was interrupted by a tidal basin where the water lapped along the shore where the restaurant now stands.

When the street was completed in 1782, a ship Captain, John Harper, bought the land that is now the north side of Prince Street, which includes that warehouse on the corner. The Raw Bar building stems from the same period.

Alexandria was built to provide a port for the plantation owners of Northern Virginia. Tobacco farmers would harvest their products and then form the leaves into round bales. They would then roll the bales to Alexandria for shipment. They were called "rolling roads". Near Potomac mills there is still a road named "Rolling Road", and it was one of those "farm to market" roads.

Once the product was transported to the Port of Alexandria it was placed in warehouses until it could be loaded in an available ship. Warehouses were built all along the shoreline of the city. City maps of the 1800's show a warehouse type building at 121 South Union. Three warehouses were turned into storehouses for Union war material during the Civil War. The Northern Army confiscated all of these buildings which forced many of Alexandria's merchants into poverty.

121 SOUTH UNION STREET
OLD TOWN ALEXANDRIA, VIRGINIA
(703) 548-1785

UNION STREET
PUBLIC HOUSE

After the war, many of the warehouses were taken by Northern merchants and speculators. Others went into disrepair as their owners were either financially unable to retain the property, had died in the war or moved west. Shipping moved to other ports as the road system became more reliable and the Port of Alexandria (as well as the Port of Georgetown) slowly disappeared. During this time the warehouse district went into decay. As many of those buildings were built with unfired brick, and were not maintained with any care, they started to crumble. Wooden buildings often burned and were not insured with a local fire company. Some were torn down to make way for improvements; others were disassembled for the material. Some time during this period, the building at 121 South Union razed, and it was not until 1972 that the current building was begun.

Underneath many of the asphalt streets in the city were brick and cobblestone. Legend has it that Hessian Revolutionary War Prisoners built a number of these, such as Prince and Princess Streete. Ballast stones came off ships using them when transporting lighter loads. It is likely that these stones and other salvage material lie under the restaurant. The bricks used to make the portion of the building that holds the Raw Bar are unfired bricks. You will notice that it is crumbling in several areas, most notably along the southern wall.

121 SOUTH UNION STREET
OLD TOWN ALEXANDRIA, VIRGINIA
(703) 548-1785

UNION STREET
PUBLIC HOUSE

Chef Jesus Cordova

Chef Jesus "Jesse" Cordova studied at the Baltimore
International Culinary College and the Culinary
Institute of America. He apprenticed at the Park
Hotel in Dublin, Ireland, under the tutelage of
Masterchef Peter Timmons and has been fortunate
enough to learn from many top international chefs.

Before coming to Union Street, Jesse worked at the
Hyatt Regency on Capital Hill, Sfuzzi in
Baltimore's Inner Harbor and McCormick and
Schmick's in Reston, Virginia.

Although classically trained, he favors the foods of
his native Caribbean Islands and New Orleans
cuisine.

121 South Union Street
Old Town Alexandria, Virginia
(703) 548-1785

Seafood Stew

8 oz. Scallops
8 oz. Shrimp
6 oz. Lobster meat
8 oz. fresh fish, diced
4 oz. Butter
1 Tsp. Garlic
4 oz. White Wine
4 oz. Fish stock or Clam juice

16 oz. Heavy Cream
1 Onion, julienned
2 stalks Celery sliced
1 Cup Corn (kernels)
1 Tsp. Worcestershire
1/2 Tsp. Hot Sauce
1/2 Tsp. Old Bay
Salt & pepper to taste

Heat the butter in a large skillet.
Add the vegetables, seafood and a little salt.
Saute for 1 minute.
Add the garlic and then the Wine.
Add the fish stock.
Bring to a boil.
Remove the seafood with a slotted spoon.
Reduce liquid by half.
Add the cream and reduce by 1/4th.
Return seafood to the skillet.
Bring back to a boil.
Add seasonings.
Serve with rice.
Serves 4

UNION STREET
PUBLIC HOUSE

121 SOUTH UNION STREET
OLD TOWN ALEXANDRIA, VIRGINIA
(703) 548-1785

Carolina Cream of Crab Soup

2 oz. Butter
1/2 Onion
1 stalk Celery
1 small Leek
4 cloves Garlic
1/2 Cup Flour
1 pint Fish stock

5 oz. Clam Juice
1/4 Tsp. Cayenne pepper
1/4 Tsp. Nutmeg
1 oz, Crab Base
1 Bay Leaf
4 oz. Crab meat, Atl. Blue
    or Dungeness

Dice by hand all vegetables. Melt the butter and sweat the vegetables for about 10 minutes. Add the Garlic and cook for 5 minutes. Turn down the heat and mix in the flour. Mix in well and cook on low heat for 5 minutes. Pour in 1/2 the fish stock and blend well with whisk. Turn up the heat and add the rest of the liquid. Let come to a boil while mixing often with whip. Turn down heat and let simmer for 30 to 45 minutes. Drop Bay leaves wrapped in cheese cloth while soup is simmering. Add Crab base and seasoning. Before serving, add heavy cream or Half & Half, Sherry, Lea & Perrins, crab meat, salt and pepper to your taste.
Serves about 4

UNION STREET
PUBLIC HOUSE

121 SOUTH UNION STREET
OLD TOWN ALEXANDRIA, VIRGINIA
(703) 548-1785

Jambalaya Griddle Cakes

3 oz. Peeled Shrimp
2 oz. raw Ricew
1 Tbsp. minced green Peppers
1 Tbsp. minced Celery
1 Tbsp. minced red Peppers
1/2 Tsp. Garlic
1/2 Tsp. Olive oil
1 oz. Andouille sausage,
   grilled & chopped

1 Tbsp. chopped Parsley
1 Egg
3 Tbsp. Flour
1/2 Tsp. Lea & Perrins
1/2 Tsp. Salt
1/4 Tsp. Old Bay
1/4 Tsp. Oregano
1/4 Tsp. Paprika
1/4 Tsp. Thyme

Cook and cool the rice.
Saute the vegetables in olive oil.
Mix all the ingredients together.
Heat a skillet with a little oil and drop in 1 oz.
portions of the mixture.
Flatten slightly and cook like a pancake.
Serve with Savannah Sour Cream Relish.

UNION STREET
PUBLIC HOUSE

121 SOUTH UNION STREET
OLD TOWN ALEXANDRIA, VIRGINIA
(703) 548-1785

Savannah Sour Cream Relish

1/4 Tbsp. Onion, minced
1/4 Tbsp. stalk Celery minced
1/4 Tbsp. Green Pepper minced
2 Cloves
1 Tbsp. Water
1 Tbsp. white wine Vinegar
1 Tsp. Sugar
1/2 Tsp. Honey
1 Tsp. Salt
1/4 Tsp. dry mustard
1/4 Tsp. crushed red peppers
1/4 Tsp. mustard seed
1/4 Tsp. Tumaric

Combine all ingredients in a stainless steel pot
and simmer for 20 to 30 minutes, until liquid
is nearly evaporated.
Cool, then combine with:

4 oz. Sour Cream
1 oz. Horseradish
1 Tsp. Lea & Perrins

UNION STREET
PUBLIC HOUSE

121 SOUTH UNION STREET
OLD TOWN ALEXANDRIA, VIRGINIA
(703) 548-1785

Mahogany Sauce

1/2 Lb. Brown Sugar
1&1/3 Cups Cider Vinegar
1/2 Med. Onion, chopped
1 Garlic clove chopped
1 Tsp. Mustard seeds
1 Tsp. red pepper flakes
1 Tsp. Paprika
2 Tsp. Thyme
1 Cup Water
6 oz. crushed Tomatoes
2 oz. Apricot preserves
1&1/2 Tsp. Bourbon
1/4 Tsp. Salt

Bring sugar and vinegar to a boil.
Reduce to a simmer.
Add rest of ingredients except Bourbon,
salt and Lea & Perrins.
Reduce until syrupy and let cool.
Strain through a china cap and add the
rest of the ingredients.

121 SOUTH UNION STREET
OLD TOWN ALEXANDRIA, VIRGINIA
(703) 548-1785

Union Street's Gumbo Base

2 oz. Butter
1 Cup Flour
1/2 Onion, chopped
1/2 stalk Celery chopped
3 cloves Garlic crushed
1 Cup crushed Tomatoes
1 Tsp. red pepper flakes
2 Tsp. Thyme

2 Tsp. Oregano
2 Bay leaves
1/2 Parsley coarse chopped
1 qt. Chicken stock
2 Cups Clam juice
Shells from shrimp peeled
    for the gumbo

Sweat the celery, onions and garlic in the butter.
Reduce the heat to low and add flour a little at a time.
Cook until the roux is brown and no grease visible.
Add remaining ingredients, blend well and simmer for
about 45 min.. Strain through a china cap.

Gumbo Spice Mix

2 Tbsp. Paprika
1&1/2 Tbsp. Old Bay
1&1/2 Tbsp. cracked black pepper
1 Tbsp. white pepper
1 Tsp. Cayenne pepper
2 Tsp. Salt
1 Tsp. Thyme
1 Tsp. Oregano

UNION STREET
PUBLIC HOUSE

121 SOUTH UNION STREET
OLD TOWN ALEXANDRIA, VIRGINIA
(703) 548-1785

The Wharf

In May 1749, the Royal Govenor of Virginia signed a bill to create a new town along the Potomac River on 60 acres of land owned by the Alexander family. Fairfax county surveyor John West, Jr., assisted by a seventeen year old apprentice named George Washington, laid out the streets and lots for the new town of "Alexandria". The original lots were purchased by many historic notables, including Lawrence and Augustine Washington, John Carlyle, William Ramsey, George Mason, Colonel William Fairfax, and George William Fairfax. At the foot of King Street, the water's edge was along Water Street (later renamed Lee Street in honor of another famous Alexandria family).

119 King Street • Alexandria, Virginia
(703) 836-2836 fax (703) 836-2830

Within a decade after its founding, Alexandria developed into an important seaport. Its economy revolved around exporting the crops and selling the diverse goods from the merchant vessels arriving in port. In 1785, Colonel George Gilpin was appointed to resurvey the town and grade & pave the streets.

A 1798 engraving of Gilpin's plan for Alexandria shows the cove filled in creating the land on which the Wharf building and other warehouses were constructed. It is generally believed that the Wharf building was built sometime in the 1790's. One indication of age is the floor joists supporting the second floor were notched into the beams at both ends, a construction technique widely used before 1800.

One of the first businesses, an importer and dealer in china and crockery, the Miller Company, installed an elevator which can still be seen next to the bar at the front of the restaurant. In 1855, the owner was in debt to the State of Virginia and the building was sold at auction for $3000. In 1888 the address was changed to 119 King Street and sold for $4500. Another change came in 1911 with Julian T. Burke, Jr., an ancestor of the family that owns Burke & Herbert Bank at King & Fairfax Streets.

In renovating the building for restaurant use, all of the original columns and beams were preserved. Traces of a Civil War fire can still be seen in some of the wood. All of the original stone and brick interior was retained. In March 1997, the Wharf Restaurant was purchased by new owners interested in preserving the distinct character of this 200 year old building, while providing an exceptional dining experience.

The Wharf

119 King Street
Alexandria, Virginia
(703) 836-2836
fax (703) 836-2830

East Coast Cioppino

1/4 Cup Olive Oil
1/2 Cup chopped Onion
1/4 Cup chopped Green pepper
1/4 Cup chopped Mushrooms
1/4 Cup chopped Scallions
1/4 Cup minced Garlic
1/4 Cup all-purpose Flour
1 28oz. Can chopped Tomatoes
12 oz. Clam juice

12 oz. Veal demi-glaze
2 Cups dry Red Wine
1/4 Cup chopped Oysters
1/8 Tbsp. Salt
1/8 Tbsp. pepper
1/8 Tbsp. Crushed red pepper
1 Bay Leaf
1/4 Cup chopped Parsley

- Saute Onions in olive oil until softened
- Add mushrooms, scallions, garlic and continue cooking
- Dust remaining vegetables in flour and incorporate.
- Add remaining ingredients and bring to a boil.
- Lower the heat and simmer for 1 hour.

2 Lobsters 1&1/4 lb.ea.
   split in 1/2 & cleaned
8 jumbo Shrimp

12 P.E.I. Mussels
8 Cherrystone Clams
12 large Sea Scallops

Place all seafood in large saute pan and cover with the sauce.
Saute until the shrimp are pink and the clams open up.
Serve immediately.

Executive Chef Jacques Butler

The Wharf
119 King Street
Alexandria, Virginia
(703) 836-2836
fax (703) 836-2830

Baked Oysters
with Herb- Spinach Butter

24 Long Island Blue Pt.
    Oysters - 1/2 shell
1 Cup fresh Spinach
2 strips Bacon chopped
1 Lb. Butter - room temp.
2 Tbsp. chopped Parsley
1 Tbsp. Lemon juice

1 Tsp. Worcestershire
1 Tsp. Black Pepper
1 Tsp. Salt
1 Tsp. minced Garlic
1 Tsp. minced Shallots
1/4 Cup dry White Wine

- Wash spinach thoroughly
- Saute Bacon until crisp.
- Add spinach and wilt over low heat.
- Chop the spinach
- In the bowl of electric mixer
  blend all ingredients
- Form butter into a roll and wrap in wax paper
- To serve: Cut a 1/4 inch slice of the
  spinach butter and place on each oyster.
- Broil oysters until butter begins to bubble.

Executive Chef Jacques Butler

The Wharf
119 King Street
Alexandria, Virginia
(703) 836-2836
fax (703) 836-2830

For 16 years, Jean-Francois and Francoise Chaufour have welcomed guests to "Le Refuge", their intimate, very romantic restaurant in the heart of Old Town. The ambience evokes the French countryside, and the delicious food completes the feeling of actually being there! While savoring "Mousse de fois de Canard Maison au Cognac" or "Escargot avec tomates eb des, ail at persil" select from an extensive wine list. Delicious French cuisine worth returning for, again and again!

Chef Jean- Claude LeLan started in the restaurant business at age 14 in his native La Rochelle, France. At "Chez Serge" he apprenticed and learned the art of pastry-making at "Le Notre". From there Chef Jean-Claude was lured to "Moveable Feast" in Sacramento, California.. From there he came to the D.C. area at "Chez Froggy" in Crystal City and "Le Vieux Logis" in Bethesda. Jean-Claude has been the Chef at "Le Refuge" for 9 years

127 North Washington Street • Alexandria, Virginia
(703) 548-4661

Duck Liver Mousse

16 oz. Duck Liver
8 oz. Butter
1 Egg
1/2 Tsp. Gelatin
1 Tsp. Salt
1/4 Tsp. Black Pepper
1 Tsp. Port Wine
1 Tsp. Brandy

Blend the duck liver for 5 min. in robot coupe.
Strain the duck liver.
Soften the Butter and put in blender with the egg
and the gelatin disolved in 2 spoons of warm water.
Add the salt, pepper, Port and brandy.
Add the duck liver and pour into terrine mold.
Cook in a bain-marie for 45 minutes at 375°.
Remove from oven and chill in fridge at least 1 day.
Serve in slices with pickles and toasted sliced french
bread.

Chef Jean-Claude Le Lan

127 North Washington Street • Alexandria, Virginia
(703) 548-4661

Chocolate Mousse Cake

10 oz. Semi-sweet Dark Chocolate
5 oz. Heavy Whipping Cream
1 Tsp. unflavored Gelatin
1 Tsp. Vanilla Extract
1 Tsp. Lemon Extract
5 whole Eggs
3&1/2 oz. Sugar

Melt Chocolate in bain-marie or double boiler.
Melt Gelatin in 3 Tbsp. of warm water.
Mix eggs and sugar in bain-marie for 5 minutes.
Pour egg and sugar mixture in mixer and blend 10 min.
Add the Gelatin, whipped cream and melted chocolate.
Pour mixture into terrine or mold and
refrigerate for overnight or at least 12 hours.

Chef Jean-Claude Le Lan

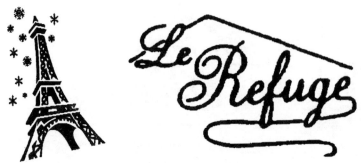

127 North Washington Street • Alexandria, Virginia
(703) 548-4661

Stabler Leadbeater Apothecary Shop
ALEXANDRIA, VIRGINIA

The Stabler-Leadbeater Apothecary Shop

In 1792, Alexandria was a bustling Potomac port city of about 300 homes. It was in that year that Edward Stabler, a young Quaker pharmacist, rented a three-story brick building on Fairfax Street and started a family business which operated continuously for 141 years. When the Depression forced the Shop's closing in 1933, the doors were simply locked.

Most of the original herbs, potions and paper labels remain in their drawers. For example, drawer #59 contains witch hazel, an age-old remedy introduced by Native Americans for external treatment of inflammatory conditions. Early pharmacists learned to value Native American remedies such as Dandelion (diuretic), Virginia Snakeroot (gastric stimulant) and Sassafras (cold remedy).

The Stabler-Leadbeater Apothecary Shop has withstood the rigors of the War of 1812, the 1821 Yellow Fever Epidemic, the Civil War (1861-1865), the Spanish-American War (1898) and World War I. Each experience brought new medical discoveries like quinine, analgesics, sulfa drugs and vaccines.

105 - 107 South Fairfax Street • Alexandria, Virginia

703-836-3713

Alexander, the Old Town Mouse

Alexander Montgomery Mouse has a most impressive background. His mouse ancestors were some of Alexandria's most respected citizens. From the pages of his children's book, "Alexander, the Old Town Mouse", you can see such names as Emma Lee, Char Lee, Whit Lee, and Will Lee !

In his book, Alexander teaches children about his very special town by visiting some of his favorite places.

As he is considered by some of his mouse friends to be one of Old Town's great chefs, Alexander has chosen to share two of his recipes with us.

With thanks to Cheryl Shaw Barnes, author and illustrator of "Alexander, the Old Town Mouse", a native of Alexandria who combined her background in architecture and love of Old Town's historic buildings to create a marvelous book for children. Her extensive research of colonial design appears throughout the book in the furniture, costumes and home decoration.

Old Town Mouse's Macaroni & Cheese

2 Cups elbow Macaroni
1/4 Cup Butter
1/4 Cup A-P Flour
2&1/2 Cups Milk

1 Tsp. Salt
1/2 Tsp. Pepper
2 Cups shredded cheese
3 slices Bread

Cook pasta about 5 minutes and drain. In a saucepan melt butter over medium heat. Blend in flour, salt and pepper. Add milk gradually while stirring. Bring to a boil while stirring constantly, until sauce thickens. Remove from heat and stir in 1&3/4 cups of the shredded cheese until it's melted. Add the cooked macaroni. Pour macaroni mixture into 2 quart greased casserole dish. Crumble bread slices on top of the macaroni. Sprinkle with the remaining 1/4 cup of the shredded cheese. Bake, uncovered, in a 375° oven for 25 to 30 minutes until browned and bubbly. Serves 4-6.

Alexander's Colonial Corn Fritters

2 Cups Sweet Corn
1/4 Cup Milk
1/3 Cup Flour
1 Egg, beaten w/ fork

1/2 Tsp. Salt
1/4 Tsp. Pepper
2 Tbsp. Butter
2 Tbsp. Oil

Combine first six ingredients in bowl. Blend together. Melt butter & oil in skillet, med. heat. Add corn mixture by rounded spoonfuls. Cook ffitter 3 to 4 mins. until golden brown on bottom. Flip with spatula and repeat for other side. Drain on paper towels. Makes about 10 to 15 fritters.

Chef Alexander M. Mouse

Alexander's recipes courtesy of
Cheryl Shaw Barnes

Cate's Bistro

Cate's Bistro opened in Old Town Alexandria in September of 1992 and has been a success on King Street ever since, calling itself the "Italian bistro with a French flair" ! A charming, cozy bistro with a comfortable feel at lunch or dinner.

<u>Chef Mario Posatta</u> has apprenticed with Cate herself, Francesco Abbruzzetti, a traditional Roman chef. Mario's mentor is Jacques Pepin, the famous French chef of television and books.

Cate's Bistro
715 King Street
Old Town, Alexandria, Virginia
703-549-0533

Tortellini ala Boscaiola

1 qt. Heavy Cream
1/2 stick Butter
2 Cups sliced Mushrooms
1 Cup diced crisp Bacon
1/2 Lb. fresh Spinach
    washed & patted dry

1/2 Cup Cognac
dash of Nutmeg
2 Lbs. Fresh Tortellini

Gently cook Tortellini in boiling water for about 5 minutes. Drain and set aside (Do Not Rinse !)

Sauce:

    Heat cream and butter in a large saute pan.
    Bring to a medium boil.
    Add rest of ingredients.
    Simmer uncovered for 7 to 10 minutes.
Add the Tortellini and toss gently.
Serve immediately in warmed dish, with some fresh Italian bread.
Serves 4

Buon Appetito !

Chef Mario Posatta

Cate's Bistro

715 King Street
Old Town, Alexandria, Virginia
703-549-0533

Elysium

According to *Conde Nast Traveler* (January 1998),
Morrison House is "one of the best places to stay
in the whole world. This '...American Federal
treasure' is for those who 'appreciate
fine things'. The formal restaurant 'serves the
best food around', and staff are 'all class'".

An elegant 45-room inn, the Morrison House
interior displays fine detailing in all public areas,
including a marble floor in the foyer, classic
parquet wood floors in the parlor and library,
crystal chandeliers and sconces, and period furnishings in each room. The guest rooms are an
elegant blend of early American charm with
modern American convenience.

In 1994 The Morrison House unveiled its new
restaurant, Elysium. Elysium is the Greek word
for paradise. The restaurant offers both the
casually elegant and romantic Elysium Dining
Room and the Elysium Grill, with it's
cherrywood and red leather and live piano entertainment Thursday-Sunday evenings.
Afternoon Tea is served Wednesdays and Sundays
in the beautiful Parlor and the Library.

Elysium
Restaurant at Morrison House

116 South Alfred Street
Alexandria, Virginia
(703) 838-8000

Elysium

Executive Chef Christopher Brooks

English-born Chef Christopher Brooks brings to the Elysium Restaurant and Morrison House a unique blend of Classical French training and years of experience in English country inns and Relais & Chateaux establishments in England and the United States. He comes from The Old Drovers Inn, Dover Plains, N.Y. where he headed their internationally recognized restaurant. Brooks had cooked and directed in some of the world's most prestigious establishments, including the Blantyre, Lenox, MA; Duxford Lodge Hotel, Duxford, England; Foxhills Golf, Leisure and Country Club, Surrey, England and the Chewton Glen Hotel, New Milton, Hampshire, England.

Chef Brooks considers himself an "enlightened traditionalist", presenting food and classical finesse with a contemporary respect for a light hand in sauces. "Food should be fun, though delivered with a proper respect for performance and presentation. As far as I'm concerned, my staff and I are on stage whenever someone enters the restaurant".

Elysium
Restaurant at Morrison House

116 South Alfred Street
Alexandria, Virginia
(703) 838-8000

Gratin *of* Chesapeake Bay Crab

with Pink Grapefruit

1/4 Tsp. chopped Ginger
15 oz. Jumbo Lump Crab
2 Pink grapefruits segmented
for the Sauce:
2 oz. Olive Oil
1 oz. Crab meat
2 oz. chopped Fennel

3 Cardamon seeds
2 chopped Tomatoes
1 clove Garlic crushed
1 lg. sprig Thyme
100 ml White Wine
300 ml Water
100 ml whipped Heavy Cream

In a large saucepan, heat olive oil and add 1 oz. Crab meat and cook for 3 min.. Add fennel, cardamon, tomatoes, garlic and thyme. Cook for another 3 mins. Add wine and water, simmer for 45 mins. and strain the stock and reduce in a clean pan until you are left with about 50 ml of concentrated crab stock. Allow to cool.

Warm the Crab meat in a pan and add ginger, season to taste with salt & pepper. Arrange pink grapefruit segments in a gratin dish and cover with the crab meat. Mix the concentrated crab stock with the whipped cream and season to taste with salt & pepper. Pour over the crab meat and place under a hot broiler for 2 minutes. Serve immediately.

Serves 4

Executive Chef Christopher Brooks

Elysium
Restaurant at Morrison House

116 South Alfred Street
Alexandria, Virginia
(703) 838-8000

Breast of Chicken
with Vegetable Goulash & Sweetcorn Pancakes

4   8 oz. boneless Chicken breasts
For the Pancakes:

4 oz. cooked Sweetcorn	1 Egg
150 ml Milk	3 oz. Flour
4 oz. Sour Cream	Salt & pepper

Mix milk, sour cream, egg and flou by hand or blender. Add sweetcorn and salt & pepper to taste. Heat a non-stick pan and measure out small pancakes with a tablespoon and saute until golden brown on both sides.

For the Vegetable Goulash:

2 oz. diced onions	1/2 Green pepper chopped
2 lg. Tomatoes skinned and diced	1 clove Garlic, crushed
	1/2 Tsp. Rosemary chopped
1 Zucchini chopped	1/2 Tsp. Marjoram chopped
1/2 Red pepper chopped	

Saute onions in nonstick pan till translucent. Add peppers, zucchini and tomatoes. Stir in garlic & herbs. Cover & simmer for 5 mins until tender. Season to taste & serve.
Reheat pancakes in oven, place on bottom of plate, top with vegetable goulash and top with roasted or grilled Chicken breast.

Executive Chef Christopher Brooks

Elysium
Restaurant at Morrison House

116 South Alfred Street
Alexandria, Virginia
(703) 838-8000

Bakewell Tart

(serves 8-10)

For the Sweet Dough

2 Cups Sugar	1 whole Egg
3 sticks Butter	1 Yolk
unsalted, soft	3 Tbsp. Milk
pinch of Salt	

Cream butter & sugar. Add eggs and milk. Slowly add flour and mix until dough comes together & is smooth. Wrap in plastic wrap & chill for several hours.

For the Almond Cream:

2 sticks Butter, soft but not melted	1 Cup almond flour(very finely ground almonds)
1 Cup Sugar	5 Eggs

Cream butter & sugar, add almond flour & mix 30 seconds. Add eggs one by one & mix til all are fully incorporated. Let mixture chill several hours.

Grease tart ring & roll sweet dough 1/4" thick. Shape into tart shell & chill. Bake shell 5 mins. at 350° til lightly browned. Remove & let cool. Once cool spread thin layer of raspberry jam on bottom of shell. Spread almond cream mix on top evenly. The almond cream mixture should be about 1/3 to 1/2 inch high. Bake at 350° for about 30 minutes. Turn the tart halfway through the baking time.

Executive Chef Christopher Brooks

Elysium
Restaurant at Morrison House

116 South Alfred Street
Alexandria, Virginia
(703) 838-8000

250th Birthday Cake Competition

Winning Recipe by Ruth Poole

Alexandria Hot Cocoa Cake

2 Cups Sugar	1 Cup Buttermilk
1/2 Cup Butter	3 Cups Flour
1/2 Cup Oil	2 Tsp. baking powder
2 Eggs	2 Tsp. baking soda
4 Tbsp. Cocoa Powder	1 Cup boiling Water

for the Icing:

1/2 Cup Butter	1 Tsp. Vanilla
8 oz. Cream Cheese	3 Tbsp.(heaping) Cocoa Pwdr.
1 box Powdered Sugar	Ice Water

Beat together the sugar, butter and oil. Add eggs and Cocoa. Keep mixer running continuously while adding buttermilk. In another bowl, mix flour, baking powder and baking soda. Mix well and blend into the batter, then add the boiling water. Blend thoroughly and pour into two 8 inch or 9 inch greased cake pans.
Bake at 350° for about 30 to 35 minutes or until a toothpick comes out clean. Remove cake from oven and let the cake cool. Top with icing. For icing, stir together all ingredients and add ice water until mixture is spreading consistency. Frost between layers and then sides and top of cake.

Judges overwhelmingly voted for this cake as the <u>Best in Show</u>, praising its texture, taste and appearance. This cake recipe originated by family members in Eastern Virginia as "the cake" for important celebrations and was carried westward by settlers. By coincidence, Mrs. Poole's daughter discovered the same cake recipe was used by her in-laws in Oklahoma as their special event cake! This confection is also incorporated as one of the layers in the Carlyle House cake that was a winner in another category.

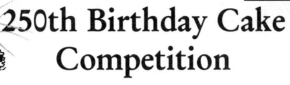

250th Birthday Cake Competition

sponsored by the

250th Anniversary Commission

Best in Show
"Alexandria Hot Cocoa Cake"
Winning Baker: Ruth Poole

Student
"Potomac River Cake" and "Crew Cake" (Tie)
John Yeingst and Will Yeingst

Home Baker
1st Place - Suzanne Slack Camden
2nd Place - Beth Barnes
3rd Place - Lauretta Kendrick

City Employee
1st Place - Wanda Dowell, Dir.Fort Ward Museum
2nd Place - Liz Milner, Office of Historic Alexandria
3rd Place - Sallie Wheeler, Fort Ward Museum

Non-Profit
1st Place - Ruth Poole, Carlyle House
2nd Place - Jeanie Fulks, the Lyceum

Creativity Award
1st Place - Tom Witte, Friends of Alexandria Archaeology
2nd Place - Carlyle House, Laura Mae Sudder
3rd Place - Kathleen Schramm, City of Alexandria

Gadsby's Tavern Museum

Since the mid 1770's, travelers have come to the tavern buildings adjoining the Market Square in Alexandria, first as guests of the tavern and hotel and now as visitors to the historic buildings. Gadsby's Tavern consists of two buildings, the ca. 1770 tavern and the 1792 City Hotel. The buildings are named for Englishman John Gadsby who operated them from 1796 to 1808. Mr. Gadsby's establishment was a center of political, business, and social life in early Alexandria.

The tavern hosted many social events, dancing assemblies, theatrical and musical performances and meetings of local organizations. It also served as a gathering place for the residents of Alexandria, a site for merchants selling their wares, and traveling dentists treating patients, plus entertainment of all description.

Gadsby's Tavern Museum
134 North Royal Street
Alexandria, Virginia
(703) 838-4242

Gadsby's Tavern Museum

George Washington frequently enjoyed the hospitality provided by tavern keepers Mary Hawkins, John Wise, and John Gadsby. General and Mrs. Washington attended the annual Birthright Ball held in his honor in 1798 and 1799. Other prominent individuals were entertained here, including John Adams, Thomas Jefferson, James Monroe, and the Marquis de Lafayette.

After serving until the late nineteenth century as tavern and hotel, the buildings went through a variety of commercial uses and fell into disrepair. In 1929, the American Legion Post 24 purchased the buildings, saving them from demolition. In 1972, the buildings were given to the City of Alexandria, restored and reopened for the 1976 Bicentenial Celebration. The museum has been fortunate to receive generous support from the community, especially the Alexandria Association and local chapters of the Daughters of the American Revolution. The staff continues to add to the Museum collection, and gifts of appropriate objects or funds are always welcome.

Today visitors are invited to tour the historic rooms of both buildings, restored to their eighteenth-century appearance. Archaeological excavation, paint analysis, and research of surviving documents have provided an accurate picture of the furnishing and use of the buildings in the period 1770-1810. A subterranean ice well is visible beside the buildings, and an early-American-style restaurant serves visitors in three of the tavern rooms. The Museum charges a small admission fee.

Gadsby's Tavern Museum
134 North Royal Street
Alexandria, Virginia
(703) 838-4242

Ecco is a true neighborhood restaurant, where Old Towner's gather to see each other as well as to dine on some of the best dishes to be found anywhere. And don't be surprised to be taking half of your dinner home with you! The portions are huge. Presided over by Co-Owner, Diana Damewood, Ecco has got to be among the friendliest places you've ever been. When you visit there a second time, Diana will probably have remembered your name. The scene of many parties, Ecco is as formal or informal as you wish it to be.

Chef Dominique D'Ermo

From the time when, as a sixteen year old boy, he fought in the French Resistance during World War II, until today, Chef and Co-Owner Dominique D'Ermo has led a fascinating life. His restaurant, Dominique's, in Washington, D.C., was a meeting place for the rich and famous, whose autographed photos line the walls at Ecco. He has written several books and has a line of soups you will find everywhere from the supermarkets to gourmet food shops.

Chef Jose (Luna) Vasquez

Dominique's recipes are beautifully executed at Ecco by master Chef Jose (Luna) Vasquez.

220 North Lee Street • Alexandria, Virginia
(703) 684-0321

Sea Scallops with Spinach, Goat Cheese & Caviar

24 oz. Spinach leaves, stemmed & cleaned	4 oz. fresh goat cheese
1 Tsp. Salt	2 cloves diced Garlic
Fresh ground pepper	24 oz. Sea scallops, shelled
4 oz. Fish stock	2 Tbsp. Butter
2/3 Cup dry white wine	4 oz. red or golden Caviar

Put spinach in a 4&1/2 qt. saucepan. Season with salt & pepper and add fish stock and 4 Tbsp. of the wine. Place pan on moderate heat and cover. When just starting to boil, lift lid and stir. Cook until just wilted, about 2 mins. Drain spinach over a bowl to catch liquid, then transfer spinach to processor & add goat cheese. Chop until the spinach & cheese are incorporated adding enough of the reserved liquid to make a very thick sauce. Add garlic and blend together. Taste for seasoning.

Heat non-stick saucepan on moderate heat, melt butter and add scallops and brown slightly on both sides. Add rest of wine and boil for 1 minute. Turn over scallops, remove from heat and let finish cooking for 2 mins. uncovered.

To serve, place spinach mixture around plate. Place scallops at center of plate. Top each scallop with a dash of the pan sauce and garnish each with a dab of caviar.

Serves 8. (If there's time, fried spinach leaves make a lovely garnish. Also a touch of grated Parmesan is good, too.)

Chef Dominique D'Ermo

ECCO CAFE

220 North Lee Street
Alexandria, Virginia
(703) 684-0321

Skillet Roasted Lemon Chicken

2 Tbsp. Ex Virgin Olive oil
1 large Lemon, sliced
1/2 Tsp. grated Lemon rind
1 Tbsp. Lemon juice
1/2 Tsp. Salt, divided
1/2 Tsp. Pepper, divided
4 Garlic cloves, minced
8 Chicken thighs, skinned
     & boned

1/4 Tsp. dried Rosemary
12 Cherry Tomatoes
12 Kalamata Olives
12 Baby Zucchini slices
8 small red Potatoes
3 Garlic cloves minced
Rosemary sprig

Preheat oven to 450°. Coat a 10 inch cast iron skillet with 1 Tsp. oil. Arrange lemon slices in a single layer on bottom of skillet. Combine 1 Tsp. olive oil, lemon rind, lemon juice, 1/2 Tsp. salt, 1/8 Tsp. pepper and 2 garlic cloves in a large bowl. Add chicken and toss to coat.
Arrange chicken in a single layer on top of lemon slices.
Combine remaining olive oil, salt, pepper, chopped rosemary, cherry tomatoes, olives, potatoes, zucchini, and 2 garlic cloves in a bowl and toss to coat.
Arrange the mixture over the chicken.
Top with a sprig of rosemary if desired.
Bake at 450° for 1 hour or until chicken is done.

Chef Dominique D'Ermo

ECCO
CAFE

220 North Lee Street
Alexandria, Virginia
(703) 684-0321

Creme Brulee

1 Vanilla Bean
1 quart Heavy Cream
1/2 Cup Sugar
6 large Egg Yolks
1/2 Cup packed dark Brown Sugar

Preheat oven to 300°.
Cut Vanilla bean length-wise, scrape out black seeds and add the cut bean to the cream. Bring to a boil. Remove from heat, cover and let the flavor go through the cream. Combine sugar and egg yolks and blend well, until yolks are pale yellow and slightly thickened. Slowly whisk the hot cream mixture into the yolk mixture. Strain thru a fine sieve into a 2 quart pitcher and skim off any foam. Place six 5 oz. ceramic or glass Creme Brulee molds in a baking pan with 2 inch sides. Add enough water to reach half way on the sides of the molds. Add vanilla cream mixture to the molds.
Bake for about 30 minutes, just for the creme to be set, but still trembling........Do Not Overbake The Custard !
Refrigerate for at least one hour or more. Remove from the refrigerator and sieve the brown sugar over the top. Glaze the molds under the broiler for a few seconds until the sugar forms a crust. Do not burn.
Serves 6

Chef Dominique D'Ermo

ECCO CAFE

220 North Lee Street
Alexandria, Virginia
(703) 684-0321

Taragon Cream Sauce

3 Tbsp. Butter
2 large Shallots, minced
2 cloves Garlic minced
1/4 Cup dry White Wine

2 Tbsp. Lemon juice
1/2 Cup Chicken stock
1/4 Cup Heavy Cream
3 Tbsp. minced fresh Taragon

Heat the butter in a medium size, heavy sauce pan over medium heat. Add the shallots and garlic and saute until they are just transpapent, but not browned, about 5 to 8 minutes. Add the wine, lemon juice and chicken stock and bring to a boil over high heat. Continue to boil until the liquid is reduced to about 1/2 cup.
Adjust the heat to low and stir in the cream and taragon. Heat through and serve immediatel.

Yield: about 1 Cup

Chef's note: The anise flavor of Taragon can perk up the delicate flavor of roast or poached chicken. Or try this sauce with grilled, baked, or poached fish. Spoon a little onto the plate and place the meat or fish on top. Then just a dollop more on top will accentuate the dish without masking its own flavor.

Chef Dominique D'Ermo

ECCO
CAFE

220 North Lee Street
Alexandria, Virginia
(703) 684-0321

Linguine with Wild Mushrooms

*(This dish must be made at the last minute, but
it's simple and takes only minutes to prepare)*

1 Lb. fresh Wild Mushrooms
(morels, chanterelles or shiitakes)
1/2 Cup Walnut Oil
1 Shallot, minced
1 clove Garlic, minced
Salt & pepper to taste

1 Cup Heavy Cream
1 Tbsp. Sherry
1 sprig Thyme, stemmed
1 sprig Taragon, stemmed
1 Tsp. chopped Basil
1 Lb. fresh Linguine

Clean the mushrooms under cold water and drain on paper towels. Slice thickly and set aside.

Place the walnut oil in a saute pan or skillet over high heat. When oil is hot, add the sliced mushrooms and saute, stirring constantly, until barely tender. Add the shallot, garlic, salt and pepper and saute another minute. Add the cream, sherry and herbs and let the sauce simmer for 2 minutes to blend the flavors.

Meanwhile, cook the pasta until just *al dente*, not too soft. Drain and toss with the hot mushroom-cream sauce.
Serves 4

Chef Dominique D'Ermo

ECCO
CAFE

220 North Lee Street
Alexandria, Virginia
(703) 684-0321

Fettuccine with Tomatoes, Basil & Garlic

5 Garlic cloves minced
4 Tbsp. chopped Basil
1 Cup sliced Mushrooms
1&1/2 Cup heavy Cream

4 Tomatoes, peeled, seeded and sliced
1&1/2 Lbs. Fresh Fettuccine
Salt & pepper to taste
1/3 Cup grated Parmesan

Bring a large pot of salted water to a boil. While the water is heating, combine the garlic, basil, mushrooms and cream in a heavy sauce pan. Bring the mixture to a boil and simmer gently, stirring frequently, until the sauce is reduced by one-third and is thick enough to coat the back of a spoon. Turn off the heat and add the tomatoes to the sauce, stirring well to blend.

Cook the pasta until it is just *al dente*. If the pasta is very fresh, it should cook in less than a minute. Drain the fettuccine well, and toss it with the sauce. Add the salt and pepper, sprinkle with the freshly grated Parmesan cheese, and serve at once.

Serves 4

(Serve this as a first course, or for luncheon with bread and a salad.)

Chef Dominique D'Ermo

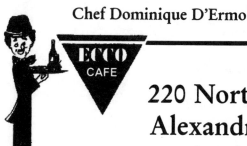

ECCO
CAFE

220 North Lee Street
Alexandria, Virginia
(703) 684-0321

The Seaport Inn

The Seaport Inn is Alexandria's first restaurant, built before 1765 ! The second owner was Colonel John Fitzgerald, George Washington's Military Aide during the American Revolution. Following the war, sails were made in the upper floors for the great sailing ships that called at the Port of Alexandria.

<u>Chef Carlos Zelaya</u>

Carlos Zelaya has been at the Seaport Inn for more than 13 years. In 1998, he was appointed Head Chef at the restaurant. Prior to coming to Seaport Inn, he was Head Chef at The Alamo Restaurant, Bullfeathers and Heidleberg restaurants.

**6 King Street
Alexandria, Virginia
(703) 549-2341**

Stuffed Trout

10 oz. Fresh Brook Trout, deboned
3 oz. chopped Spinach
2 oz. Baby Shrimp
2 oz. Backfin Crab meat
2 oz. shredded Mozzarella cheese
2 Tbsp. melted Butter
1/3 Cup fresh Lemon juice
1/4 Cup White Wine

Combine spinach and shrimp and stuff the trout.
Layer crab meat and cheese on top.
Add Lemon juice and wine to the butter.
Ladle juice/wine/butter sauce over trout.
Broil 4 inches from heat for 8 to 10 minutes.
Serves 1

Chef Carlos Zelaya

The Seaport Inn

6 King Street
Alexandria, Virginia
(703) 549-2341

Bouillabaise

Marinara Sauce:
Combine the following ingredients and set aside.

> 3/4 Cup Tomato Sauce
> 1/4 Cup chopped Tomatoes
> Basil, Oregano, Salt & Pepper to taste.

Bouillabaise:

1 Tbsp. Oil	3 - 6 oz. fish filet or steak pieces
3 oz. 26/30 Shrimp	2 oz. chopped Red pepper
3 oz. Sea Scallops	2 oz. chopped Green pepper
2 oz. chopped Clams	2 oz. chopped Onion
3 oz. King Crab Legs	1 oz. minced Garlic
3 pcs. Top Neck Clams	5 oz. Marinara Sauce
3 oz. Mussels	Oregano, salt & pepper

Heat oil in saute pan. Saute seafood and fish with garlic for about five minutes. Add marinara sauce and vegetables. Simmer for about ten minutes.

Chef Carlos Zelaya

The Seaport Inn

**6 King Street
Alexandria, Virginia
(703) 549-2341**

Boyhood Home of Robert E. Lee
Alexandria, Virginia

Boyhood Home
of
Robert E. Lee

For the serious historian or the casual visitor, the boyhood home of Robert E. Lee is a must to see. Situated in the Old and Historic Alexandria District, this elegant mansion was the home of Confederate General Robert E. Lee for most of his boyhood years. Tastefully and artistically furnished with authentic period pieces, this stately Federal townhouse was the site of frequent visits by George Washington. Here also the Marquis de Lafayette paid a formal call on Ann Hill Carter Lee, the mother of General Lee and the widow of General "Light Horse Harry" Lee of Revolutionary War fame.

In the drawing room Mary Lee Fitzhugh married George Washington Parke Custis, grandson of Martha Washington, and builder of Arlington. Twenty-seven years later, their daughter, Mary ann Randolph Custis became the wife of Robert E. Lee.

607 Oronoco Street • Alexandria, Virginia
(703) 548-8454

Portner's Restaurant is located at 109 South St. Asaph Street in the heart of Old Town Alexandria.

The building was originally constructed in 1883 by the Columbia Fire Company #4, which occupied it until 1960. The present establishment takes its name from the Robert Portner Brewing Company which was located on St. Asaph Street in the nineteenth century.

Portner's Restaurant reflects the Victorian heritage of a city rich in history. In the 1800s the Portner's building housed Columbia Fire Company No. 4, which boasted one of the city's first steam fire engines. One hundred years later the building became the home of one of Old Town's finest restaurants, taking its name from the Robert Portner Brewing Company, which was located on the Northern end of St. Asaph Street. When the building was purchased, it was in need of restoration. Blending the character of the old brick building with modern times began with extensive research in 19th century architecture. The demolition of a period home in Baltimore ended six months of searching for bricks to match the original burgundy-colored ones. These perfected the façade, which at one time had a two-arch exterior. The interior wall is constructed of bricks from the old Alexandria reservoir.

Chef Edwing Flores

Before coming to the USA, Chef Edwing Flores taught philosophy, ethics and history in his native El Salvador. In this country he turned his talents to cooking and has had a successful career in Washington, D.C. at the Shoreham Hotel, the Washington Hilton, the Capital Hilton, the Sheraton Carlton and the famous "Jockey Club" at the Fairfax Hotel on Embassy Row. Edwing came to Virginia to work at the Evans Farm Inn in McLean, then to R.T.'s in Arlington. His cuisine has been delighting customers at Portner's since 1997. He also found time to run his own "Flores Bakery" for a couple of years.

109 S. St. Asaph Street
Alexandria, Virginia
703-683-1776

Pecan Pie

4 10" pie shells	¼ tsp. Salt
5 cups dark Karo Syrup	4 TBL. Vanilla
5 cups Sugar	8 cups Pecans
12 Eggs	1 cup Flour
2 cups melted butter	4 oz. Chocolate shavings

1. Blend syrup, sugar, salt and vanilla in mixing bowl for 2 minutes.
2. Add butter and mix 2 more minutes
3. Add eggs and flour and mix for 30 seconds (do not over whip)
4. Put 2 cups of pecans in each pie shell
5. Sprinkle 1 oz. Of chocolate over each pie
6. Divide filling evenly over 4 pies.
7. Bake at 325 for 50-60 minutes.

Yeild: 4 pies

Chef Edwing Flores

109 S. St. Asaph Street
Alexandria, Virginia
703-683-1776

Spicy Rosemary Tuna

Tuna Fish Steak
Rosemary Marinade
Mashed potatoes
Mixed vegetables
Chopped parsley
White wine

1. Place Tuna in marinade overnight.
2. Mark on grill and set on hot plate.
3. Pour wine over it. Cook to desired doneness.
4. Place mashed potatoes in center of plate.
5. Arrange Tuna leaning on potatoes and place vegetables around other side of potatoes.
6. Pour 1 Tbsp. Of Rosemary marinade over tuna.
7. Garnish with parsley

Chef Edwing Flores

109 S. St. Asaph Street
Alexandria, Virginia
703-683-1776

Rosemary Marinade

15 oz.	Garlic Chili Puree
2 bunches chopped	Fresh Rosemary
2 cups	Vegetable Oil
2 cups	Teriyaki sauce
2 TBLS. Chopped	Fresh ginger

Mix all together.

Dill Sauce

2 Qt. Heavy Cream	2 tsp. Chicken Base
½ cup Puree Onion	¼ cup Cornstarch
1 cup White Wine	½ cup Water
1 bunch Fresh chopped Dill	

1. Place onion and wine in sauce pan and boil.
2. When reduced by ½, add cream and heat completely.
3. Add base and cornstarch and dissolve.
4. Finish with dill when desired thickness is reached.

Chef Edwing Flores ,

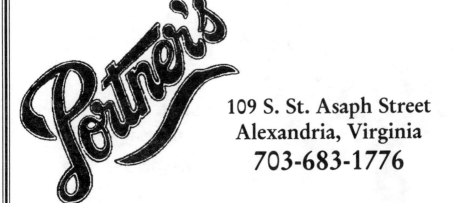

109 S. St. Asaph Street
Alexandria, Virginia
703-683-1776

Broiled Salmon with Dill Sauce

8 oz.	Salmon Filet
2 oz.	10% Oil
2 oz.	White Wine
5 oz.	Capellini
5 oz.	Mixed Vegetables
A.N.	Salt and Pepper
4 oz	Dill Sauce
1 Tbsp.	Chopped parsley

1. Place salmon over oiled hot plate.
2. Pour wine, salt and pepper over salmon.
3. Place under broiler for 3 minutes, then move to oven and bake 4-5 minutes.
4. Heat pasta and vegetables in hot water, then place on round plate
5. Place salmon on top of pasta vegetable mixture, top with Dill Sauce
6. Garnish with chopped parsley

Chef Edwing Flores

109 S. St. Asaph Street
Alexandria, Virginia
703-683-1776

Hoisin Sauce

1 #5   Hoisin Sauce
1 cup Soy Sauce
1 cup Sesame oil
3 TBL Orange juice
4 oz   Lime juice
3 cups Honey
1 cup White sugar
1 cup Brown sugar
3 TBL Garlic
8 oz   Chili Puree

1. Place all ingredients in sauce pot and boil.
   Reduce heat and simmer for 5 minutes
2. Strain in china cup

Yield: 3 ½ Quarts

Chef Edwing Flores

109 S. St. Asaph Street
Alexandria, Virginia
703-683-1776

Friendship Firehouse

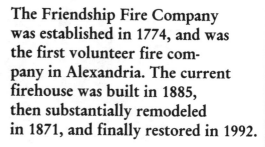

The Friendship Fire Company was established in 1774, and was the first volunteer fire company in Alexandria. The current firehouse was built in 1885, then substantially remodeled in 1871, and finally restored in 1992.

The first floor engine room features hand drawn fire engines, buckets, axes, hose and other historic fire-fighting apparatus. Exhibits in the restored second floor meeting room feature the elaborate Victorian furnishings typical of the period. Also on view are ceremonial objects, such as parade uniforms, capes, banners and other regalia.

The tradition of George Washington's association with Friendship Fire Company, honored by Friendship members for nearly 200 years, is celebrated in several historic images of Washington throughout the museum.

107 South Alfred Street
Alexandria, Virginia

Open 10 A.M. to 4 P.M. Friday & Saturday
1 P.M. to 4 P.M. Sunday

Virginia Beverage Company is Old Town's premier restaurant and brewery. We pride ourselves on our unique combination of southern cuisine and hand-crafted beverages in an atmosphere that fits our Old Town address.

Chef Paul Maher's daily specials ensure something new and different every visit. Brewer Jason Oliver's recipes have quickly become quaffable favorites of the casual and avid beer fan alike.

Located at 607 King Street in the heart of historic Old Town, enjoy a relaxing dinner in the warm and inviting dining room. Try the Sunday lunch buffet, too. Stop by for a cigar while enjoying a libation from an extensive list, or take a tour of the brewery and learn about the trade.

VIRGINIA BEVERAGE COMPANY
RESTAURANT & BREWERY
607 KING STREET ● ALEXANDRIA, VIRGINIA
(703) 684-5397

Chef Paul Maher
Virginia Beverage Company

Chef Paul Maher grew up in New Jersey where he learned the basic recipes and techniques of fine cuisine from his mother and grandmother. He then continued his education at the New England Culinary Institute in Vermont, quickly learning to combine his formal training with the simple country cuisine that he loves.

Paul further expanded his abilities, discovering traditional southern cuisine under Chef Carter Echols at Sutton Place Gourmet. "Working with Chef Echols opened my eyes to the same "living off the land" philosophy that I enjoy so much more from my more native New England cuisine. It's the synergy of necessity and art that, to me, makes food great."

Paul begins with familiar, traditional recipes and makes them a new experience. Everyone has a favorite Bar B Que recipe: here Paul takes one of his and adds housemade rootbeer for a unique but somehow familiar flavor.

VIRGINIA BEVERAGE COMPANY
RESTAURANT & BREWERY
607 KING STREET • ALEXANDRIA, VIRGINIA
(703) 684-5397

Rootbeer Bar B Que

1 Onion, finely diced
2 qt. Root beer
1 can Katsup
1/2 Cup Cider Vinegar
1 Cup Worchestershire
1/2 Lb. Brown Sugar
1/2 Cup Molassas
1 Tbsp. Salad Oil

Saute onions in the oil over medium heat until deeply caramelized. Add the root beer and bring to a boil and reduce by 1/4th.
Add remaining ingredients, bring to a boil and simmer for 30 minutes.

Chef Paul Maher

VIRGINIA BEVERAGE COMPANY
RESTAURANT & BREWERY
607 KING STREET • ALEXANDRIA, VIRGINIA
(703) 684-5397

Florida Bar B Que

2 Oranges	1/2 Tsp. Allspice
1 Lemon	1 Tbsp. Tomato Paste
1 Lime	2 Habanero pepper,
1/2 Cup dry White Wine	fresh roasted
1 Tsp. Ginger fresh grnd.	1 Tbsp. Rice Wine Vinegar
1/2 bunch Thyme	1 Tsp Salad Oil
1 Clove Garlic, smashed	

Roast the peppers in a hot (400°) oven with a little oil until golden brown. Cool the peppers in an airtight container. When completely cool, remove seeds and as much skin as possible. Wear disposable gloves as the oil from the peppers is HOT!. Puree the peppers with the vinegar until smooth. Wash the citrus and juice them into a sauce pan. Cut the peels into quarters and put in pan as well. Add Thyme, Wine, Ginger, Garlic and Allspice. Reduce by half. Strain the liquid and add the Tomato Paste and 1/2 the Habanero puree.
Taste and adjust seasoning with salt if necessary. To turn up the heat, add remaining puree.

Chef Paul Maher

VIRGINIA BEVERAGE COMPANY
RESTAURANT & BREWERY
607 KING STREET • ALEXANDRIA, VIRGINIA
(703) 684-5397

Chefs Serge and Wendy Albert

The menu of Tempo reflects the diverse backgrounds and culinary preferences of Serge and Wendy Albert. Written in French, Italian and English, the dishes represent Serge's classical French training in Toulouse and experiences in Washington's Italian restaurants, and Californian Wendy's "New American" cuisine with flavors of the Southwest. They elect to keep their establishment in this rather nondescript section of Alexandria called Strawberry Hill because it enables them to keep menu prices considerably lower than a more fashionable location and has enough free parking available for all their clients.

4231 Duke Street • Alexandria, Virginia
(703) 370-7900

Chocolate Zucchini Cake

6 Cups Grated Zucchini	2 heaping Tsp. Baking Soda
4 Cups Sugar	2 Tsp. Vanilla
3 Cups lite Vegetable oil	2 Cups sifted Cocoa
8 Eggs	1 Cup Pecans (optional)
4 Cups all-purpose Flour	

Preheat oven to 325°. Butter and Flour three 9" round cake pans. Whip sugar and oil in mixer at high speed until blended. Add 1 Egg at a time, beating until light and fluffy. Add Zucchini, flour, baking soda and cocoa. Mix on low until blended. Add Vanilla and nuts. Bake for 1 hour. Completely cool the cakes. Slice each layer in half so you have six layers. Each cake will consist of three layers. Frost with Chocolate Cream Cheese Frosting and assemble.

Combine and blend until creamy:
>   1/2 Lb. Butter
>   1/2 Lb. Cream Cheese
>   1&1/2 Lbs. powdered Sugar
>   1 Tsp. Vanilla
>   1 Cup sifted Cocoa

Serge & Wendy Albert, Chef/Owners

4231 Duke Street • Alexandria, Virginia
(703) 370-7900

Beef Medallions with Roquefort

8 medallions of Beef Tenderloin 3 oz. each
1 Tsp. vegetable oil
2 Tsp. Dijon Mustard
2 oz. Dry White Wine
3 oz. Roquefort cheese
1 Cup heavy whipping cream
Salt & Pepper to taste

In a large saute pan, heat the oil. Lightly salt & pepper the beef medallions.
When pan is hot, add medallions with salted side down. Sear on both sides to your desired degree of doneness.
Remove the medallions and place on serving tray.
Add Dijon mustard and wine to the pan. Deglaze the pan by gently rocking while scraping the bottom with a wooden spatula until the liquid is reduced. Now add the roquefort and the cream. Reduce until the sauce covers the back of a spoon.
When the sauce has reached the desired consistency, spoon a little over each medallion. Garnish with a pinch of chopped fresh Parsley.

(Note: Sauce also works well to dress up hamburgers or sauteed Chicken breasts.)

Serge & Wendy Albert, Chef/Owners

4231 Duke Street • Alexandria, Virginia
(703) 370-7900

Torpedo Factory Art Center

In 1974, the City of Alexandria and a group of local artists formed a unique partnership to renovate a former World War II munitions factory into one of the nation's finest working centers for the visual arts. Today the Torpedo Factory Art Center houses 200 professional artists in 80 studios and galleries, an art school, and an archaeology laboratory and museum.

Over 750,000 people visit annually, to watch artists at work in such diverse disciplines as pottery, fiber arts, painting, sculpture, jewelry making, printmaking, and intrument making.

In 1982, a group of citizens, recognizing the importance of the arts to the well-being of our community, strengthened the partnership by forming the Friends of the Torpedo Factory Art Center, Inc., a 501(c)3 charitable organization.

Friends of the Torpedo Factory Art Center
105 North Union Street • Alexandria, Virginia
(703) 683-0693

IRELAND'S OWN

RESTAURANT & PUB

Many years ago, proprietor Pat Troy left his native Offaly, Ireland and journeyed to America to make his fortune. In 1974 he opened his gift shop, The Irish Walk, and next his restaurant and pub in Old Town, which has become a focal point for much of the Irish community in metropolitan Washington, D.C.

Pat hosts a radio broadcast "Pat Troy's Irish Radio Show" every Sunday, and he can be found most nights at Ireland's Own entertaining and delighting guests with "zany spirits" and "unicorn antics".

132 North Royal Street
Alexandria, Virginia
(703) 549-4535

Bacon 'N Bushmills Clubsteaks

4 8 oz. Club Steaks or
    filet mignons
Sea Salt
fresh ground Pepper
8 slices Irish Bacon
1/4 Cup Bushmills
1 Cup Beef stock
1/2 Cup Heavy Cream

Season well both sides of meat with salt and pepper.
Drizzle Bushmills Irish whiskey over steaks.
Wrap each steak or filet with a slice of Irish bacon,
and secure with a toothpick.
For medium rare steaks, saute over high heat in a
lightly oiled pan for about 5 minutes.
Pour remaining whiskey into the pan and flambe.
Remove steaks and keep warm.
Add beef stock to pan and scrape any browned bits.
Add cream and bring to boil. Reduce until thick
and serve over steaks on heated plates.
Serves 4

Chef George Nasibi

IRELAND'S OWN
RESTAURANT & PUB

132 North Royal Street • Alexandria, Virginia
(703) 549-4535

Shepherd's Pie

1 Lb. ground Beef
2 Tbsp. chopped Onion
1/4 cup diced cooked Carrots
1/4 cup peas
8 oz. Beef Gravy
1 Lb. mashed Potatoes
1 Egg beaten
Salt & pepper to taste

Combine the ground beef, chopped onions, cooked diced carrots and peas in an oven-proof casserole dish.
Pour the beef gravy over the mixture and top with the mashed potatoes.
Brush potato topping with the beaten egg.
Place in broiler until top is golden brown.
Can also be made in individual serving dishes.
Serves 4

Chef George Nasibi

IRELAND'S OWN
RESTAURANT & PUB

132 North Royal Street • Alexandria, Virginia
(703) 549-4535

The Lyceum

The Lyceum is Alexandria's History Museum. Originally built in 1839 as a community cultural center and library, this elegant Greek Revival structure still serves as an educational and cultural focal point.

An on-going exhibition tells the story of Alexandria, founded in 1749 and once one of the busiest ports in America. Using archaeological finds, old photographs, maps, original art and a wide variety of historic artifacts, visitor's explore the city's past. Smaller changing exhibits in the Coldsmith Gallery let visitors focus on specific people, places or events within Alexandria's history.

The Lyceum's Lecture Hall, where philosophers, politicians and scientists have spoken since before the Civil War, still hosts a variety of public activities for all ages. The Lyceum Museum Shop offers many excellent books, prints, toys and historic reproductions, allowing you to carry some of Alexandria's past home with you.

- Located in the heart of Old Town Alexandria's shops and dining
- Minutes from Washington, D.C.
- Open seven days per week, Mon-Sat, 10-5; Sun, 1-5; closed New Year's, Thanksgiving and Christmas.
- No admission, free parking
- Tour bus to Mt. Vernon

The Lyceum—Alexandria's History Museum
2021 South Washington Street
Alexandria, Virginia 22314
Phone: 703 838-4994
Fax: 703 838-4997
e-mail: lyceum@ci.alexandria.va.us
web: http://ci.alexandria.va.us/oha

Potowmack Landing
Restaurant

16 June 1608

"....the River of Potowmack. Fish so thicke with their heads above water. For want of nets (our barge driving amongst them) we attempted to catch them with a frying pan; but we found it to be a bad instrument to catch fish with. Neither better fish, nor more plenty, had any of us ever seen in any place so swimming in water."

Almost 380 years have passed since Captain John Smith entered that observation in his log as he sailed past this island. The mighty Potomac still courses almost 400 miles from tiny streams in Garrett County down over Great Falls, past Potowmack Landing, and out into Chesapeake Bay. The Piscataway, Susquehanna and Seneca Indians are gone now, and a great city has grown on the shores and in the once wild forests. But the mighty river whose name means "they are coming by water" and "river of swans" remains.

Steeped in the lore of American history, the Potomac played a key part in America's expansion and trade all over the globe. The Port of Alexandria lured shipwrights and sea captains with its deep water harbor and abundance of raw materials. One of these men was Bathurst Daingerfield. A mariner by profession, Captain Daingerfield and his young wife, Eliza Kaye, settled in Alexandria in 1800. He fathered several children including John B., after whom the island is named.

Everything John B. Daingerfield touched during his long life seemed to bring success. He soon became the wealthiest man of his day in Alexandria. With his riches came an abounding charity to his fellow townspeople. He was a great benefactor to St. Paul's Church. When the town could not afford the rebuilding of the fire-razed Market House, he provided funds for the project. He presented the city with a steeple and the town clock. He died loved, honored, and remembered.

Potowmack Landing Restaurant
At Daingerfield Island
1 Marina Drive • Alexandria, Virginia
(703) 548-0001

Jumbo Lump Crab Cakes

2 Lbs. Jumbo Lump Crab Meat
1/2 Cup fresh Bread Crumbs
1 Egg
1&1/2 Tbsp. Dijon Mustard
1 Tbsp. Worcestershire Sauce
1 Ts. Tabasco Sauce
6 Tbsp. fresh chopped Parsley
1/2 Cup Mayonnaise
1 Tbsp. Old Bay Seasoning

Remove all shell and cartilage from the Crab meat. Mix together the egg, mayonnaise, parsley, Old Bay, Tabasco, Worcestershire, mustard and bread crumbs. Season to taste with salt and pepper. Carefully fold in the Crab meat making sure not to break up the nice lumps. Form into 4 ounce cakes. This can be done in advance.

When ready to serve, place on a sheet and broil until golden brown. Serve two cakes per person with Lemon wedges, Tartar sauce and cocktail sauce.

Chef Mark Giuricich

Potowmack Landing Restaurant
At Daingerfield Island
1 Marina Drive • Alexandria, Virginia
(703) 548-0001

Dark Chocolate Torte

1 Lb. Semisweet Chocolate
5 oz. Butter, room temp.
4 large Eggs
1 Tbsp. All-purpose Flour
1 Tbsp. Sugar
pinch Salt

Butter, Flour and place a parchment circle in the bottom of an 8 inch cake pan. Break the chocolate into small bits and melt in a double boiler over hot water. When almost melted, stir with a rubber spatula until smooth. Stir in the butter, a third at a time, completely incorporating the first third before adding the next. Set aside to cool slightly. Meanwhile, separate the eggs. Beat the egg yolks at high speed for 5 minutes, add the flour and beat for 1 more minute. In a separate bowl beat the egg whites to soft peaks with the sugar. In a large mixing bowl gently fold the egg yolks into the chocolate mix. Do not mix completely. Gently fold 1/3 of the egg whites into the mix. Once it has been incorporated, gently fold in the remaining egg whites until blended. Turn into the prepared pan and rotate the pan gently in each direction to level the batter. Bake for 15 minutes at 425°. Remove from oven. The center will appear raw. This is OK. Cool on a rack for 1 hour. Run a knife around the edge of the pan to loosen the torte. Remove the paper and cover with a plate and invert. When completely cool, wrap with film and chill for service. Cut into 16 slices. Dust with powdered sugar, a dollop of whip cream and serve with sliced strawberries.

Chef Mark Giuricich

Potowmack Landing Restaurant
At Daingerfield Island
1 Marina Drive • Alexandria, Virginia
(703) 548-0001

Quickie Chicken Cacciatore

1 whole Chicken cut in pieces
1 - 2 Tbsp. Vegetable Oil
1 can Stewed Tomatoes
1 8 oz. can Tomato Sauce
1 envelope powdered Spaghetti Sauce mix
1 Tbsp. Brown Sugar
dash Salt & pepper

Pre-heat oven to 350°
Brown chicken in oil in heavy skillet.
Arrange chicken in baking dish.
Combine remaining ingredients.
Pour over chicken.
Cover tightly with foil.
Bake in oven for 1 hour, or until chicken is tender.
Serve with pasta or rice and a vegetable or salad.
(Note: recipe also works well with pork chops.)

Chef Kerry Donley

City of Alexandria, Virginia
Kerry J. Donley,
Mayor

Mount Vernon

Mount Vernon, the home of George Washington, is owned and maintained by the Mount Vernon Ladies' Association, the oldest historic preservation organization in the United States.

Founded by Ann Pamela Cunningham of South Carolina, the association might never have come into existence were it not a tradition for ships to toll their bells when passing Mount Vernon. When in 1853 her mother was summoned to deck by such a bell, ringing in homage to the nation's first president, she was horrified at the sight of the once grand house in a state of complete disrepair.

Cunningham launched a campaign to raise funds to purchase and preserve Mount Vernon. The country responded and five years later the Mount Vernon Ladies Association purchased the buildings and 200 acres surrounding from John Augustine Washington, Jr., a great grand-nephew of Washington's. Under the Association's 140 year long trusteeship, it has been restored to its original appearance.

Today Mount Vernon is a national monument, open to the public every day, serving over 1,000,000 visitors annually.

Bread Pudding

4 Cups day old white or
   French bread cubes
   crusts removed
1/2 Cup seedless raisins
3 Tbsp. melted Butter
4 Eggs
1 Tsp. Cinnamon

1/2 Tsp. Nutmeg
1/2 Tsp. Salt
2/3 Cup Sugar
3 Cups Half & Half
1&1/2 Tsp. Vanilla
Sweetened Whipped Cream

Arrange bread cubes and raisins in buttered 1&1/2 quart baking dish or casserole and drizzle with butter. Combine eggs, cinnamon, nutmeg, and salt, beating slightly. Dissolve sugar in the milk and add to egg mixture in a fine stream, stirring constantly. Stir in the vanilla.

Pour over bread crumbs and bake in a moderate oven (350°) for 55 to 60 minutes, or until a silver knife inserted in center comes out clean. Serve slightly warm or chilled, plain or with sweetened whipped cream.

Mount Vernon Ladies' Association

No tax dollars are expended to support Mount Vernon: The Association does not accept grants from the federal, state or local government. The mansion and its grounds, outreach and education programs, and estate events and activities, are supported through the generosity of patriotic individuals, foundations and corporations, together with in come from gate receipts and gift shop and restaurant income.

www.mountvernon.org

Mango Mike's

COOL CARIBBEAN CAFE

When you're in the mood to get away to an unusual eating experience, Mango Mike's is sure to draw you near with its wonderful spicy cuisine and island-type setting. Consider also its award-winning reputation. The Restaurant Association of Metropolitan Washington named Mango Mike's the "Best New Restaurant for 1996". Washingtonian Magazine listed Mango Mike's in the top 100 "Best Bargain Restaurants" for 1997 & '98.

The Caribbean, Cuba, the Florida Keys and Latin America are the inspirations for and influences on Mango Mike's menu, which also features the chef's own Neuvo Latino creations. House specialties include Jamaican "jerk" Chicken, Cuban Roast Pork with Orange and Red Onion Glaze, Key West Crabcake, Conch Cake with Rum and Pepper Shrimp, Bermuda Bread Pudding with Jamaican Rum Sauce. A mainstay since 1985, the Spicy Seafood Gumbo is rich and thick with shrimp, crabmeat, oysters and andouille sausage. As for the décor, think banana trees and murals; palms and a flowering of hibiscus plants on the outdoor deck.

Chef Andres has been with Mike for 15 years. He has encountered many different styles in this time which has influenced and helped mold his unique style. Andres says, "I like to taste the spice". He's only 32 years old, so we hope to continue to taste the spice for many years to come.

Mango Mike's

320 N. Pegram Street • Alexandria, Virginia
(703) 823-1166

Mango Mike's Seafood Gumbo

Vegetables:
3/4 Cup Onion chopped
1/2 Cup Green Peppers, chopped
1/3 Cup chopped Celery

Seasonings:
1 Bay leaf
1 Tsp. Salt
pinch White Pepper
pinch Cayenne pepper
pinch Black pepper
pinch dried Thyme
1/2 Tsp. dried Oregano

for the Roux:
1/4 Cup Vegetable oil
1/4 Cup A-P Flour
1 Tsp. minced Garlic

for the Seafood:
1 Cup Clam juice
1 Cup Water
6 oz. Andouille sausage cut in 1/2 inch pcs.
8 med. Shrimp peeled & deveined
5 med-lg Oysters scrubbed
4 oz. Back fin Crabmeat

In a mixing bowl, combine onion, bell peppers & celery.
In separate bowl mix all seasonings together, set aside.
In a large skillet over high heat, add oil until it is almost
at smoking point(4-5 mins.). Gradually add flour, whisking constantly until the roux takes on a reddish brown
color(about 2-4 mins.). Immediately add the vegetables
and cook for 2 minutes. Add the Garlic and cook for 1
more minute.

In a large saucepan, bring water and clam juice to a boil
and add the roux and vegetable mixture, one spoonful
at a time. To the sauce pan add the seafood and sausage
and cook until it boils, and then serve.
Serves 6

Chef Andres

320 N. Pegram Street
Alexandria, Virginia
(703) 823-1166

Mango Mike's
COOL CARIBBEAN CAFE

Mango Chipotle Ketchup

6 Tbsp. Vegetable oil
3 diced red Onions
9 ripe Mangos peeled
   & diced

1&1/2 Cups Brown Sugar
1&1/2 Cups red wine Vinegar
8 Chipotle Peppers
3/4 Cup Molasses

Heat oil in large saucepan. Add onion & saute until soft. Add remaining ingredients & bring to a boil. Simmer for 1 hour. Transfer mixture to food processor, season to taste with salt & pepper and puree until smooth.

Chimichurri

3 oz. fresh Garlic
1 whole Jalopeno,
   coarsely chopped
1&1/2 Tbsp. Salt

1/2 Cup chopped Parsley
2 Tbsp. chopped Oregano
2 Tbsp. dist. Vinegar
3 Tbsp. Olive Oil

Clean parsley, remove stems and chop. Do the same with the Oregano. Process the Garlic, Jalopeno with enough vinegar to make smooth. Add the chopped Parsley, vinegar, oregano, salt and oil and process until thoroughly mixed.

Chef Andres

320 N. Pegram Street
Alexandria, Virginia
(703) 823-1166

Mango Mike's
COOL CARIBBEAN CAFE

Brown Sugar Pound Cake

2 sticks Butter
1/2 Cup Crisco shortening
5 Eggs
1 Lb. and 1 Cup Light Brown Sugar
3&1/2 Cups Flour
1/2 Tsp. Baking Powder
1 Cup Milk

Let butter and eggs "sit" until they're room temperature. Cream together 2 sticks of butter and 1/2 cup of Crisco. Add the 5 eggs one at a time, creaming after each. Add 1 Lb. and 1 cup of brown sugar. Sift together 3&1/2 cups of plain flour and 1/2 teaspoon of baking powder. Add this flour/baking powder mixture , alternately with 1 cup of milk to the sugar mixture.
Bake in a greased and floured tube pan for 1&1/4 to 1&1/2 hours in a 325° preheated oven.

for the frosting:

1 stick Butter   1 Box Confectioner's Sugar
1 Cup chopped Pecans   Milk to thin

Toast chopped pecans in 1 stick butter in thick broiler pan until they brown well. Let cool a little, then add confectioner's sugar. Add milk enough to thin to a spreading consistency. Spread on top of cake. Some should "drip" down the sides and center, but should not be spread anywhere except on top.

Celebrity Chef Willard Scott

NBC's "Today" Show

& good 'ole Virginian !

Good luck and great success with the cookbook.
All good wishes to you, and God bless.

Willard Scott

New Virginia Cuisine

Located at the top of Old Town Alexandria, across from the King Street Metro station, Stella's Restaurant serves New Virginia cuisine by Chef Peter Myers. The retro supper-club style dining room is a perfect setting for pleasant dining on any occasion. In the spring and summer months their fountain patio offers fine dining al fresco. They offer validated parking evenings after 5 pm.

Executive Chef Peter Myers apprenticed under Chef Peter Harmon in Sanibel, Florida before being recruited by the Hilton Corp. to run their operation in the Berkshire mountains of Mass. It was in search of new challenges that led to New Orleans' Ponchartrain Hotel and a passion for Cajun and Creole cuisine. Lured from there to Alexandria by Capital City Entertainment Group, he opened Crescent City Restaurant and then Fleetwood's Blues Club as Exec. Chef. His background and mastery of many different cuisine styles has amde him an instant hit in Alexandria where he has deftly blended traditional Virginia cuisine with contemporary preparations and ingredients.

1725 Duke Street • Alexandria, Virginia
(703) 519-7610

Pinenut & herb Crusted Rainbow Trout with Saffron roasted Garlic Aioli

4 10 oz. boneless Rainbow Trout
1/2 Gal. fresh Bread crumbs
1/2 Cup chopped Parsley
1/4 Cup Garlic fine chop
1 Cup fine chop Pine nuts
2 Tbsp. Salt
1 Tbsp. Black Pepper
1 Cup A/P Flour

4 Eggs whipped
Vegetable Oil

1/2 Cup peeled Garlic cloves
1/3 Cup red wine Vinegar
1/2 Tbsp. Saffron
2 Egg Yolks
2 Cups Olive oil
Pinch salt & pepper

Rinse Trout skin well. Combine bread crumbs, parsley, garlic, pinenuts, salt and pepper. Dust Trout evenly with flour and then coat evenly with eggwash. Bread the skinless side of the fish evenly and saute in the vegetable oil until lightly golden brown. Turn over onto skin side and bake for 5 minutes in a 350° oven.

For the Sauce: Roast the garlic with a little veg. oil covered with foil at 350° until soft. Bring saffron & vinegar to boil, then cool to room temp. Combine garlic, vinegar, saffron, yolks, salt & pepper in processor. Add olive oil in a stream to emulsify.

Executive Chef Peter Myers

Stellas *New Virginia Cuisine*

1725 Duke Street • Alexandria, Virginia
(703) 519-7610

Clyde's at Mark Center celebrates the sporting life on the water in its two bars - the Straight Wharf Bar and the Crew Bar - and three dining rooms. This casual gathering place offers something for everyone including 10 microbrews on tap, margaritas, steaks, seafood, pasta dishes, burgers, seasonal specialties such as wild Alaska salmon and locally grown fruits and vegetables, and a menu for children. The Oyster Bar serves an array of the finest oysters from the East and West Coasts and award winning wines. Sunday brunch is a specialty.

Opened in 1998 in Alexandria's West End, Clyde's at Mark Center is part of the locally and privately owned Clyde's Restaurant Group, one of the nation's most innovative and enduring restaurant companies. Each restaurant is unique, and all are dedicated to providing exceptional food, service and value.

Executive Chef George Chaffman
A graduate of L'Academie de Cuisine in Bethesda, he has worked for Washington's only Michelin Two Star Chefs. Banquet Chef for Jean-Louis Palladin at the Watergate Hotel 1993-1995, and Sous Chef under Gerard Pangaud at Gerard's Place from 1995 to late 1997, when he arrived at Clyde's in Georgetown.

1700 N. Beauregard Street • Alexandria, Virginia
(703) 820-8300

Clyde's Spinach Salad

8 Cups Spinach leaves
  washed & spun dry
8 Halves Deviled Eggs
1 Cup croutons

1/4 Cup crumbled Feta
1/4 Cup crumbled Bacon
4 oz. Bacon Dressing
Salt & pepper to taste

Toss the spinach & croutons with the bacon dressing and place in a serving bowl. Garnish dish with Feta cheese, crumbled Bacon and spiced Walnuts. Place deviled eggs around salad. Makes 4 servings.

Clyde's Bacon Dressing

1 fine minced Shallot
1/2 Lb. Bacon crumbled
3 oz. Sour Cream
2 oz. red wine Vinegar

6-7 oz. Salad & olive oil
1 Clove fine minced
Salt & pepper to taste
1 Tsp. (rounded) Mustard

Cook bacon until very crisp & drain. Combine crumbled bacon with shallots, eggs, garlic, vinegar, mustard and salt & pepper to taste in a mixing bowl. Slowly whip in the oil to make the emulsion. Fold in the Sour Cream.

Executive Chef George Chaffman

Clyde's
at
Mark Center

1700 N. Beauregard Street • Alexandria, Virginia
(703) 820-8300

Clyde's Spiced Walnuts

1 Cup Walnuts
1/3 Cup sugar
1 pinch Cinnamon
1 pinch Ginger
1 pinch Nutmeg
1 pinch Cream of Tartar
1 pinch Cayenne pepper
1 Tbsp. water

Preheat the oven to 375° and toast the walnuts
for about 5 minutes until fragrant.
Cook remaining ingredients until the syrup
reaches the soft ball stage (235° on a candy
thermometer)
Add the walnuts and toss to coat.
Remove from heat and allow to cool.
Season with salt.

Executive Chef George Chaffman

at
Mark Center

1700 N. Beauregard Street • Alexandria, Virginia
(703) 820-8300

Maine Mussel Chowder

with Saffron, White Potato Mousselene and Red Pepper Pesto

8 Lbs. Mussels
4 sliced Shallots
4 smashed Garlic cloves
2 Cups White Wine
4 sprigs Thyme
2 Cups diced Potatoes
1 Cup Leeks, white part
2 Cups diced Celery Root
1&1/2 qts. Fish stock

Bouquet garni (Taragon, thyme
    parsley stems, fennel seeds,
    bay leaf)
4 Roma tomatoes peeled,
    seeded & julienned
1 pinch Saffron
2 Tbsp. Sherry
2 Tbsp. Chives

for the Red Pepper Pesto:
        2 Red peppers peeled, seeded
        2 Tbsp. Ex Virgin olive oil
        1 Tbsp. Pine Nuts
        1 Tbsp. Parmesan cheese

recipe continues on next page......

Executive Chef George Chaffman

Clyde's at Mark Center

1700 N. Beauregard Street • Alexandria, Virginia
(703) 820-8300

Maine Mussel Chowder, Red Pepper Pesto, White Potato Mousseline

for the White Potato Mousseline:
Combine 4 Cups of mashed Potato with 2 Tbsp.. of
roasted garlic puree and 1/2 cup of Heavy Cream.
Pipe into center of the bowl.

In a shallow pot place mussels, shallots, garlic(raw),
thyme, white wine and steam until mussels open.
(don't over cook)
Remove mussels and discard shells. Strain liquid &
reserve to make the chowder.
Sweat leeks in butter with the b.g., saffron and cook
till translucent. Add thickened Fish stock and simmer
for 10 minutes. Add potatoes, celery root and cook till tender.
Just before serving, heat chowder base along with cooked
mussels, tomato julienne and finish with the Sherry.
Ladle into a flat bowl, pipe roastes garlic mousseline of
potato in the center and top with red pepper pesto. Finish
with a sprinkle of freshly chopped Chives.
Serves 4.

Executive Chef George Chaffman

1700 N. Beauregard Street • Alexandria, Virginia
(703) 820-8300

Moran's Delectable Dip

(This delicious snack can be made to feed as little as one
during late study hours, or as many as twenty-five for a Super Bowl party.)

1 soft Avocado
1 Lb. grated Cheese
1 avg.size container Cottage Cheese
1 medium size Tomato
1 pkg. Chili or Taco seasoning
1 large bag Nacho style chips
(This is enough for 1 or 2.)

This recipe is concerned with appearance as much as taste. It is very important to make in following order.
1. Dice the avocado in small pieces and spread on bottom of a clear dish. The avocado should cover bottom.
2. Next, dice the Tomato & spread on top of avocados.
3. The following layer is grated cheese.(save some for top)
4. Next, add 3/4's of the seasoning to the sour cream. Mix well until blended. The sour cream should take on a pinkish tint. Spread sour cream on top of cheese layer. This is actually tricky, the object is not to disturb the cheese.
5. As the finale, the remainder of the cheese should be sprinkled on top

Chef James Moran

Hon. James P. Moran
Congress of the United States
House of Representatives
8th District of Virginia

murphy's'

a grand irish pub

713 King Street
Alexandria, Virginia
(703) 548-1717   fax 739-4583

Irish Potato Cake

1/2 Cup shortening
1 Cup warm mashed Potatoes
1/2 Tsp. Salt
1 Cup nuts or coconut
2 Tsp. baking powder
2 Cups Flour

2 Cups Sugar
1 Tsp. Soda
1 Tsp. Vanilla
1/2 Cup Milk
2 Tsp. Cocoa
4 Eggs separated + 2 yolks

After preparing the rest of the mixture, beat the
4 Egg whites and fold into the mixture.
Bake at 350° for 30 minutes.

for the Frosting:
1 Cup Milk
1 Cup Sugar
1 Tbsp. Butter

1 Cup Coconut
2 Egg yolks beaten
1 Tbsp. Flour

Combine all ingredients
Cook until it thickens
Add coconut
Spread over cake

Serves 4

Irish Meggies

2 cubes of nucco
2 cups white sugar
1 cup brown sugar
2 Eggs
2 Tsp. cream of tartar
2 Tsp. soda

2 Tsp. vanilla
1/2 cup nuts
1 cup white raisins
2 cups oats
1 Tbsp. nutmeg
3 cups flour

Combine all ingredients except flour. Add that last. Make firm dough. Make small balls and roll in orange sugar and flatten on buttered cookie sheet. Bake for 10 minutes at 350°. Makes 4 dozen small, 2 dozen large.

Irish Potatoes

1/4 Cup Butter
1/4 CupKaro light syrup
1 Tsp. Vanilla

1/2 Cup coconut
2 Cups powdered Sugar
Cinnamon

Cream together butter, syrup and then add the vanilla and coconut. Then add a little powdered sugar at a time.
Shape into bite-sized balls.
Roll the balls in cinnamon.
Put on wax paper and refrigerate overnight.
Makes 3 dozen.

Irish Soda Bread

8 Cups Flour
2 Cups Sugar
3 Tbsp. Baking Powder
2 Tsp. Baking soda
2 Tsp. cream of Tartar
2 Cups Raisins
3 Eggs well beaten
3/4 Cup melted Butter
1 Qt. Buttermilk

Mix flour, sugar, baking powder, baking soda,
and cream of Tartar in a bowl.
Add raisins and stir.
Stir in eggs and melted butter.
Add buttermilk.
With wooden spoon, mix until well blended.
Divide dough into 3 equal portions.
Lightly grease bread pans.
Bake in preheated 305° oven for 1 hour.
If not done after 1 hour, check every 5 minutes.

murphy's

a grand Irish pub
713 King Street • Alexandria, Virginia
(703) 548-1717   fax 739-4583

Santa Fe East

Foods of the Southwest.

With its inspiration as Santa Fe, New Mexico, "a place where the setting sun paints the ancient mountains, where arid breezes mingle with the desert sand and where old and new customs and traditions blend, Santa Fe East brings the flavor and ambience of the Southwest to Old Town".

Santa Fe East is located in an historic building built at the height of the War of 1812. From the outside, the building still reflects the grace, elegance & historic flavor of Old Town, with brick facade, residential windows and narrow brick alleyways. On the inside, it has been entirely redesigned to recreate the look and feel of a Santa Fe style restaurant, with Southwestern artworks and genuine Indian and Mexican artifacts.

110 South Pitt Street
Alexandria, Virginia
703-548-6900

Santa Fé East Chef/Owner David Dai

began his culinary training at an earlt age. His father was Chief Executive Chef at the famous Coffe House Restaurant in Hong Kong in the sixties and was frequently guest chef at the well-known Mandarin Hotel there.

With his inherited skill and his knowledge of the trade and his roots in French cooking, David has been Chef/Part owner of Henry's Restaurant in Bethesda and La Bonne Auberge Restaurant in Great Falls.

His interest in and interpretation of Southwestern regional cooking together with his French backround have created a totally new dining experience at Santa Fe East! In Chef David's own words, "In developing a Modern Southwestern Cuisine, I have combined the traditional ingredients, the Southwest principles and authenticity with the techniques and versatility of French cuisine".

Santa Fé East

Foods of the Southwest.

110 South Pitt Street ● Alexandria, Virginia

703-548-6900

Roasted Duckling
with Black Mole Sauce

1 Whole Duckling(4-5 Lbs.)
  cut into quarters
1 Tbsp. Sea Salt
1 Tbsp. Chile Puro
1/2 Tbsp. Chopped Garlic
8 oz. Mexican Chocolate sauce
1/4 oz. fresh Oregano
1/4 oz. Thyme

1 Cup Tamarindo Syrup
2 Cups Duck Stock
2 dry Ancho Chilies
2 dry Arbol Chilies
1 small bunch Cilantro
Black pepper
Pumpkin & Sesame seeds

Trim and save all of the duck fat for cooking the duck leg.
Debone the breast, but leave the thigh-bone intact. Rub the
duck legs with Sea salt, chile puro and ground black peppercorns. Grill the duck legs in a skillet, skin side down. Cook
until golden brown. Add the duck fat and cook on low heat
for 30 minutes.
Check duck legs by inserting a knife into the leg; when
it goes in smoothly, the duck is done.
Sear the duck breast in the skillet - medium-rare is
recommended.
For the Sauce:
Melt the Mexican Chocolate with the Duck Stock.
Combine with all other ingredients in a food processor
and blend well.
Serve sauce warm.

Chef/Owner David Dai

Santa Fé East

110 South Pitt Street • Alexandria, Virginia
703-548-6900

Mexican Chocolate Brownie

1 Lb. Ibarra Mexican Chocolate
1&1/2 Lbs. Sweet Butter
15 whole Eggs
10 Egg Yolks
10 oz. Flour
8 oz. Sugar
4 0z. Pine Nuts

For the Sauce:
12 oz. Sugar
1/2 Tbsp. Salt
1 Cup Milk
1 Qt. Heavy Cream
Few drops Vanilla Extract
Crema De Inglesia

Put the Eggs and Sugar in the mixer and set on medium speed. Blend for 15 minutes. Then put milk, chocolate and butter in the microwave and heat until the chpcolate is completely melted. Next, add the chocolate, then the flour into the egg mixture.
Pour this mixture into a sheet pan and sprinkle pine nuts on top. Bake in a 350° oven for 20 minutes.

For the Sauce:
Combine all ingredients into a double boiler for 15 minutes or until firm.
Remove from heat and cool in an ice water bed for 5 minutes.
Prepare the serving plate and spread with the sauce.
Place Brownie on top and serve.

Chef/Owner David Dai

Santa Fé East

110 South Pitt Street • Alexandria, Virginia
703-548-6900

Santa Fe Black Bean Soup

1&1/2 Lbs. Black Turtle Beans
1 White Onion
2 Cups Chopped Tomatoes
1 Tbsp. dry Basil
1 Tbsp. dry Thyme
1 Tbsp. dry Oregano
1 Tbsp. Cumin
1 Tbsp. Chipotle Chile
2 Gal.s Chicken Stock
Seasoning
Fresh Cilantro

Pour all ingredients in a soup pot and cook until beans are soft.
Then put into blender with small amount of Cilantro & blend.
Serve in heated bowl topped with sour cream and fresh tortilla chips.
Serves 10.

Chef/Owner David Dai

Santa Fe East

110 South Pitt Street • Alexandria, Virginia
703-548-6900

Sour Cream Chocolate Cake

2 Cups Sugar	1 Tsp. Salt
2 Cups Flour	4 oz. melted Chocolate
1 Cup Water	2 Eggs
3/4 Cup Sour Cream	1/2 Tsp. baking powder
1&1/4 Tsp. baking soda	1 Tsp. Vanilla

Beat all ingredients together for 1/2 minute on low speed.
Then beat on high speed for 3 minutes.
Bake at 350° in two 9 inch greased pans for 25 to 30 mins.

for the frosting:
1/3 Cup softened Butter
3 oz. melted Chocolate
3 Cup confectioners sugar

2 Tsp. Vanilla
1/2 Cup Sour Cream

Beat all together until creamy & frost cake as desired.

Celebrity Chef Vola Lawson

Vola Lawson is City Manager of the City of Alexandria

Demera
ደመራ

Demera means the eve of Meskel. The feast of Meskel has been celebrated for 1600 years in Ethiopia and commemorates the finding of the True Cross by the Empress Helena, the mother of Constantine the Great. On the day of Demera, long branches from trees are tied together. Yellow daisies, popularly called Meskel flowers, are placed at the top of the branches, forming tall pyramids. They are placed in entrances of compounds and at night they are lighted. In the capital of Addis Ababa, thousands gather at the main square to greet the season of flowers.

At Demera Restaurant in Arlington, owner Gebremeskel Kahassai has created a delightful atmosphere of comfort and friendliness.
Here you will find no forks, no knives and no desserts, but you will enjoy scooping up meats and vegetables spooned into colorful mounds on an injera-lined platter. More of these spongy, bubbly, fermented pancakes lie folded on the sides of the platter, ready to be used as your "scooper". If you have never tried Ethiopian Cusine, come try exotic-sounding dishes for breakfast, lunch or dinner. Demera is open 7 days a week from 10am until 2pm. On Fridays, Saturdays and Sundays, you can enjoy cultural Ethiopian music and dancing. A large parking lot is adjacent to the restaurant.

Authentic Ethiopian Cuisine
2325 South Eads Street • Alexandria, Virginia
(703) 271-8663

Gomen

(Collard greens)

1 lb collard greens	1 tsp ginger
1 lg red onion	salt to taste
2 green bell peppers	1 cup oil
2 tsp garlic	2 cups water

Boil collard greens ½ hour. In separate pan saute red onion, garlic, ginger, salt and pepper in oil until onion is soft. Add chopped green peppers, cook 1 minute. Add collard greens and serve. 5 servings

Doro Wot

1 cut up Chicken	2 cups water	
2 Onions	6	hard Boiled eggs
½ tsp cardamom	2	lemons
½ tsp red pepper	4 oz	red wine
2 tsp garlic	2 tsp	salt
½ tsp ginger root	1 cup	melted butter

Wash chicken parts and rub them with lemon wedges. Saute onions in butter. Add red pepper and mix it well. Add chicken pieces and cook about 30 minutes. Just before serving add hard boiled eggs and pepper to taste. 5 servings

Demera

ደመራ

Authentic Ethiopian Cuisine

2325 South Eads Street • Alexandria, Virginia
(703)-271-8663

Tibs
(beef special)

1 lb beef cubes
2 cups onions
1 cup butter
½ cup red pepper
4 buds garlic

1 tsp cardamom
salt to taste
3 jalapin peppers
4 oz. red cooking wine

In butter saute onions with peppers ad spices.
Add beef and wine and cook to your liking.
Just before serving add one tomato and remove
it instantly. For a milder dish do not use the red pepper.
4-6 servings

Misir Wot
(split Lentil dishes)

2 cups split lentils
1 lg red onion
6 cups water
1 cup oil
4 oz. red cooking wine

½ cup red pepper
1 tsp. ginger
1 tsp. garlic
6 jalepino peppers
salt to taste

Rinse lentils in water 5 min. or until soft. Saute
onions in oil and add wine, spices and salt. Add soft
lentils and 2 cups water and simmer for about ½ hour.
Serve hot or cold

Kiki Alitcha

(vegetable dish)

2 cups yellow split peas	4 oz red cooking wine
1 cup red onions	1 tsp turmeric
1 cup oil	1 tsp curry
4 cups water	salt to taste
1 tsp garlic	

Boil split peas until soft, then drain. Saute red onions, turmeric, ginger and garlic in oil.
Add wine, salt and spices. Add softened peas and heat through.

Lega Tibs

(Lamb special)

1 lb. lamb chunks	1 tsp garlic
½ sliced onion	½ tsp cardamom
1 jalepino peppers	½ tsp ginger
1 tsp. black pepper	½ cup melted butter
½ sliced green pepper	

Saute onion in butter. Add jalepinos, green pepper, and spices. Add lamb and cook until done to your taste. Just be fore serving stir in a small touch of butter.
3to 4 servings.

Demera

ደመራ

Authentic Ethiopian Cuisine

2325 South Eads Street • Alexandria, Virginia
(703)-271-8663

TRATTORIA da FRANCO

305 S. Washington St, Alexandria
703 548-9338

Franco Abbruzzetti, proprietor and chef of Trattoria
da Franco, is adventuresome and creative. Raised in
Rome during World War ll, he has many fascinating
and harrowing tales of his life in Italy and France
during that period and sometimes can be persuaded to
relate them over a glass of wine. Franco and his sister
attended the Parisian restaurant and cooking school of
the "Hotel du Lac" and worked in his Uncle Oresti's
restaurant. Franco then migrated to London and
spent 18 years, making a culinary name for himself as
chef to such notables as Queen Elizabeth and Prince
Philip, Sir Winston Churchill and Prime Minister
Harold Wilson.
In America, Franco brought his talents to the
Georgetown "Pisces Club" and later developed the
popular "Tiberio" on Washington's busy K Street.
Next he moved to the more tranquil atmosphere of
Old Town, Alexandria, when he joined "Terrazza",
then a popular restaurant on King Street. In 1985, he
opened the "Trattoria da Franco". With its authentic
Roman cuisine, traditional Italian décor and Franco's
own ebullient personality and style, it is and always has
been a favorite with visitors and natives alike. A
crowning touch for his many accomplishments, Franco
was awarded the prestigious Medal for Excellence for
1995 by the Accademia Italiana Della Cucina, one of
the highest honors in the culinary field. In additional
to his excellent cuisine, Trattoria is the home of a
monthly Opera Night, where the best of the world's
music is presented. And for those who wish to im-
merse themselves in the Italian tradition, Italian language and Italian cooking classes are offered.

Peperonata Salad

 4 Tbsp. Olive oil
 1 yellow onion peeled
      & quartered
 2 Red Bell Peppers,
      seeded & cut into
      1 inch squares
 2 Tbsp. chopped Fresh Basil
 2 Tbsp. Balsamic Vinegar
 1/4 Tsp Salt
 1/8 Tsp. Black pepper
 1   Clove Garlic chopped

Pour half of the virgin olive oil into a medium size non-stick skillet on high heat and cook almost to the smoking point. While the oil is heating, cut the onions in quarters and the garlic into very small pieces. When the oil is ready, add the onions and the bell peppers with the garlic and cook on high heat for 2 to 4 minutes. Add the fresh Basil and 1 Tbsp. of the balsamiv vinegar. Stir and cook for 30 seconds. Remove from heat and transfer to a bowl. Toss everything together until well coated and ready to be served.
Serves 4

Chef Francesco Abbruzzetti

TRATTORIA da FRANCO

305 S. Washington St, Alexandria
703 548-9338

Pappardelle all'Aragosta

2 Live Lobster ea.1&1/2 Lbs	1 oz. Butter
1&1/2 oz. olive oil	1 Cup sliced Fennel
1/2 Cup diced red Onion	1 Cup sliced Mushrooms
1/2 Cup diced Carrots	1 Bay leaf
1 clove Garlic minced	1 Chili pepper chopped
1/4 Cup diced Celery	Pinch of Saffron
1/3 Cup Grappa	1 pint Whipping Cream
1/2 Cup White Wine	6 Sage Leaves
4 Cups fresh Tomato sauce	1&1/2 Lbs. Egg Pappardelle
1 qt. Chicken Stock	

Plunge the Lobster Head Only into boiling water to kill. Place in a 450° oven for about 8 minutes & remove & cool. Separate the tail and claws from the body. Remove all flesh. Crush the lobster shell into small pieces. Heat olive oil in a heavy-bottomed 4 quart suacepan. Add the lobster for about 30 seconds over high heat. Add onions, garlic, carrots and celery & cook over moderate for 5 minutes. Add 1 Tbsp. tomato paste, 1/2 cup of Grappa. Deglaze with the wine. Add the tomato sauce, chicken stock, bay leaf, chili peppers, saffron and rest of ingredients. Continue cooking until reduced to 2 cups. Strain through a sieve and press out as much of the solids as possible. Serve over freshly-cooked ad dente pasta.
Serves 6

Chef Francesco Abbruzzetti

TRATTORIA da FRANCO

305 S. Washington St, Alexandria
703 548-9338

On the Potomac

George Washington Memorial Parkway

**9030 Lucia Lane
Alexandria, Virginia
*(703) 799-1501***

Cedar Knoll Inn

The original farmhouse that is Cedar Knoll Inn today was constructed in the late 1800s as a tenant farm house for the 115.34 acre plantation called "Marsland on the Potomac". The property included the stately main house (now known as the "Tower House" adjoining Cedar Knoll on the south, a 2-story boat house, barn and other out buildings.

Originally owned by Lawrence Washington, Marsland became the property of George Washington on June 20, 1752. From General Washington to current owners, Antonio and Beatriz Flores, it has changed hands 19 times.

In 1909 then owner Dr. Bliss was playing cards upstairs in the boathouse and lost the property in a poker game. He then moved across the river to Maryland and built a new home that is a close replica of the "Tower House".

During World War 1 the "Tower House" was used as a convalescent hospital for troops returning from the front.

In 1935 Pauline Walsh bought the property. She added a screen porch, the Log room and a second story porch, redecorated and turned it into a fashionable Antique Shop. Next owner Mildred Linster made numerous changes and additions and was the first to use it as a restaurant. It was Miss Linster who gave Cedar Knoll Inn its present name. From then until now each owner has contributed to the renovations and the result is the Cedar Knoll Inn of today, a perfect mix of the historic, delicious, romantic, the beautiful and the memorable.

In 1920 James and Ethel Drain took title and in 1930 deeded 9.461 acres to the United States of America for the building of the George Washington Memorial Parkway.

Chef Tony Flores

Tony Flores is currently the Chef/Owner of Cedar Knoll Inn on the Potomac. He brings with him 30 years of cooking experience following a long family tradition reaching back 75 years.

Tony has studied in France and at the Squola Piemontese in Torino, Italy. He has worked at The Savoy Hotel in England and at the Romeo & Juilet Restaurant in Washington, D.C. and in New York City.

Chef Flores has three beautiful daughters and he shares his love of cooking with his wife, Beatriz.

One of Tony's favorite recipes:

Veal Monte Carlo

6 oz. Of veal	1 slice of Italian ham
4 oz. Of boneless chicken breast	1 slice of Swiss cheese

Bread the veal and chicken by dipping in egg and rolling in flour and bread crumbs. Fry in butter and place on top of ham and Swiss cheese. Top with White Sauce.

White Sauce

Heat melted cream cheese, heavy cream, mushrooms and brandy until it makes a slightly thick sauce. Stirring constantly while heating. Serves 2-4 people

George Washington Memorial Parkway
9030 Lucia Lane
Alexandria, Virginia
_(703) 799-1501_

"Politically Correct Campaign Cookies"

1 Lb. Brown Sugar	1 Tsp. Baking Soda
1 Cup White Sugar	2 Tsp. Baking Powder
1&1/2 Cups Crisco	1 Cup Milk to which you add
2 Cups sifted Flour	1 Tsp. Vanilla
2 Eggs	1 Lb. dark Raisins
1 Tsp. Salt	6 Cups plain raw Oatmeal,
6 Tsps. Cinnamon	quick but not instant
1 Tsp. Nutmeg	

Put raisins inn warm water to soften and set aside. Set oven at 350°. Place first 10 ingredients in bowl with 1/2 the milk mixture and blend well. Then add remaining milk and beat until light and fluffy. Place raisins in strainer, then fold gently into mixture. Now add oatmeal, on medium speed, one cup at a time. Spray 3 large cookie sheets with Pam and drop batter by teaspoonful, allowing room to spread without touching. Bake in center of oven for 15 to 20 minutes, just until they start to turn a light brown. Overcooking will make them hard. If your oven seems a little slow, turn up to 375° but no higher. Let cookies cool a few minutes before sliding on wire rack. Be sure they've cooled completely before storing.

Chef Charles Robb

Sen. Charles S. Robb
United States Senate
Virginia

Armed Services Committee
Committee on Finance

Select Committee on Intelligence
Joint Economic Committee

Sour Cream Pound Cake

2 sticks Margarine	6 Eggs
3 Cups Sugar	1 Cup Sour Cream
3 Cups Flour	1 Tsp. Vanilla
1/4 Tsp. Baking Soda	1 Tsp. Lemon extract

Cream margarine and sugar. Add eggs one at a time. Beat well after each addition. Stir in the flavorings. Add the dry ingredients alternately with the sour cream.

Bake at 325° for 1/2 hour. Reduce heat to 300°. Bake at least another 45 minutes, usually more, until done.

Chef Patsy Ticer

SENATE OF VIRGINIA

𝔖enator 𝔓atricia 𝔖. 𝔗icer

30th District

RESTAURANT & LOUNGE

A local favorite. Serving innovative seafood, beef, poultry, and game. Complemented by seasonal vegetables and followed by heavenly house-made desserts.

A fabulous dining experience with a gracious and professional staff. Two enchanting and romantic dining rooms, complete with fireplaces.

The decor is colorful and nostalgic, filled with 50's memorabilia which one could describe as "after art deco and before avocado green appliances". Guests have described the restaurant as reminiscent of their favorite restaurants in Rehoboth, Los Angeles and Manhattan. Stardust is offbeat, stylish and cosmopolitan, while remaining comfortable and casual.

Owners John Kilkenny and Avery Kincaid are always on hand to make sure your visit is filled with "Stardust Memories" !

608 Montgomery Street
North Old Town Alexandria, Virginia
703-548-9864

RESTAURANT & LOUNGE

Executive Chef Pat Phatiphong

Chef Pat Phatiphong is from Thailand yet has worked in such bastions of fine cuisine as the Ritz Carlton, Harvey's and the Rive Gauche in D.C.. He opened the Bangkok Gourmet in the 80's and was one of the pioneers in popularizing Thai cuisine in the Washington, D.C. area.

Chef Pat has received numerous accolades, including the recent inclusion in "Chefs 2000" as one of the top chefs in the nation !

At Stardust, Chef Pat has a varied menu reflecting both his Asian heritage and his vast international experience. His dishes are presented with great flair and color that has now become his signature.

RESTAURANT & LOUNGE

608 Montgomery Street
North Old Town Alexandria, Virginia
703-548-9864

115

Whole Grilled Rockfish

1&1/4 to 1&1/2 Lbs. cleaned whole Rockfish
3 oz. Butter
2 Tbsp. Capers
2 Tbsp. white Vermouth
1 Tbsp. chopped Shallots
1 Tbsp. Lemon Juice
Pinch of Salt & Pepper

Place a sprig of fresh Rosemary inside the fish.
Season with Salt & Pepper.
Score fish.
Cover and grill outside over the coals or
Bake in a 450° oven for 12 to 15 minutes.

Melt butter in sauce pan.
Saute Shallots until clear.
Add Capers, Vermouth and Lemon juice.
Pour Sauce over fish and serve.

Executive Chef Pat Phatiphong

STARDUST
RESTAURANT & LOUNGE

608 Montgomery Street
North Old Town Alexandria, Virginia
703-548-9864

Shiitake Mushroom & Napa Cabbage Consomme

1   quart Vegetable Stock
8   oz. Napa Cabbage
1 Lb. Shiitake mushrooms
4   oz. Soy Sauce
2   Spring Onions, chopped
Salt & White Pepper to taste

Chop napa cabbage length-wise.
Bring vegetable stock to a boil.
Add Napa Cabbage and shiitake mushrooms.
Cook until mushrooms are tender.
Add Soy sauce and salt & pepper to taste.
Serve in heated bowl and top with chopped
spring onions.

Executive Chef Pat Phatiphong

608 Montgomery Street
North Old Town Alexandria, Virginia
703-548-9864

"I Got the Blues" Salad

12 oz. Mixed Baby Lettuces
4 oz. Blueberries
4 oz. Blackberries

2 strips Applewood Smoked
    Bacon, crumbled

Gorgonzola -Blue Dressing:
8 oz. non-fat Yogurt
3 oz. crumbled Gorgonzola
2 oz. Buttermilk
1/2 Tsp. Dry Mustard
Worcestershire Sauce(to taste)
Tabasco Sauce (to Taste)

For the Dressing:
Combine all ingredients in a mixer bowl or
food processor. (25 Cal., 1 g. fat)

Cook and crumble the bacon.

Build salad with the greens.
Add the berries, the crumbled bacon and
top with the dressing.

(it's lo-fat and lo-cal & you'd never know it !)

This salad is amazingly easy and amazingly delicious!
It's so good you'll forget your blues !

Janet Poleski, Chef/Instructor

 # Azalea Catering

"Gourmet with a Southern Accent"
Phone (703) 922-5985
Fax (703) 549-4614

Crabmeat, Avocado & Shiitake Quesadilla
with Dancing Mango Salsa

1 Cup Jumbo Lump Crabmeat picked over for shells
2 Avocado chopped fine
1 Cup Shiitake Mushrooms, sliced
4 oz. Canchopped Green Chilis
1 Cup chopped green Onions
1/2 Cup chopped Red Pepper

1 Cup diced Ripe Tomatoes
1 Lb. grated Monterey Jack
8 12 in. Flour Tortillas
Sour Cream
1 bunch Cilantro, finely chopped
Mango Salsa (recipe follows)

Saute mushrooms in olive oil and set aside. Prepare Mango Salsa now so the flavors have chance to mingle. Stir 1/2 the chopped Cilantro into the sour cream. Prepare quesadillas by layering 4 tortillas with approx. 2 oz. of cheese, crab, avocado, mushrooms, chilies, green omions, peppers and tomatoes. Sprinkle with a little more Cilantro. Add 2 oz. more of cheese on top and cover with another tortilla. Grill or saute in a large hot skillet. Cut into 8 wedges. Garnish with a small dollop of Cilantro/sour cream, top with sprig of cilantro. Serve Mango Salsa on the side.

For the Mango Salsa:
Combine in a bowl 2 Ripe Mangos, diced
1/2 small diced red Onion
1 small Jalapeno, diced
Juice from an Orange, Lemon & 2 Limes
1/4 Cup diced Red Pepper

Janet Poleski, Chef/Instructor

 # Azalea Catering
"Gourmet with a Southern Accent"
Phone (703) 922-5985
Fax (703) 549-4614

Norfolk Crab Cakes

Fresh Chesapeake Bay crab meat	Ground Black pepper
Fresh onions	Bread Crumbs
Green Bell Peppers	Heavy Cream
Parsley	Eggs
Vegetable salt	Fresh Butter

1) Pre-cook onions, taking care not to lose firmness or texture.
2) Slightly saute peppers to release full flavor.
3) Mix crab, egg, cooked onions, peppers, bread crumbs, S & P.
4) Add sufficient cream to bind the mixture lightly.
5) Saute butter til brown, add parsley & release flavors.
6) Form cakes and drop in butter, saute sparingly.
7) Remove and serve.

(Chefs note: "this is a creative recipe in which the precise measurements, preparation of the mix, and cooking variables are trade secrets known only to the chef. Traditional crab cakes are those made with a mix of the ingredients recommended above and amounts to suit the chef's particular taste.")

Chef John Warner

Sen. John Warner
United States Senate
Virginia

Chairman, Armed Services Committee

Environment & Public Works Committee
Rules and Administration Committee

RESTAURANTS

Chadwicks Restaurant, originally opened in Georgetown in 1967, has been an Old Town landmark tradition since 1979. This locally owned and operated tavern is nestled on the waterfront between Duke and Prince Streets, and is a favorite haunt for local residents. The weathered brick and warm wood interior make for a comfortable stay, whether enjoying Sunday Brunch, or just drinks by the fireplace. Chadwicks is open seven days and offers a great selection of fresh seafood, their famous crab cakes, as well as steaks, ribs, burgers and great salads.

Chef Jamison Clark
Since October of 1997, Jamison Clark's been cooking up a storm at Chadwicks. A graduate of the Culinary School of Washington, Chef Clark brought new flair to the menu at Chadwick's while retaining the classic dishes which have made Chadwick's famous. His previous appointments at Colonel Brooks Tavern, Ciao Baby, and Loew's L'Enfant Plaza Hotel have certainly broadened his culinary expertise and made him a welcome asset at Chadwick's !

203 Strand Street • Alexandria, Virginia
(703) 836-4442

Chadwick's Clam Chowder recipe has been a closely-guarded secret since they opened in Georgetown in 1967. Years may pass between visits, but guests can always count on the same great chowder. Chef Clark reveals this classic recipe for the first time, and also shares his own creative recipe for Blackened Catfish with Black Beans & Rice.

New England Clam Chowder

2 - 3 Large Potatoes peeled & diced	1/2 Tsp. white Pepper
6 oz. Butter	1/2 oz. chopped Garlic
8 oz. diced white Onion	1&1/2 Cup Flour
8 oz. diced Celery	1 qt. Clam Juice
2 oz. diced Leeks	1 oz. Clam Base
1 Tsp. dried Thyme	1 Lb. chopped Clams
1 small Bay leaf	1 qt. Half & Half

Boil the Potatoes until tender and set aside. Meanwhile, saute the onions, leeks, celery and garlic in butter until transpapent. Add the flour to the pan, cook and stir for 15 minutes over medium heayt. Add the Clam juice, clam base and seasonings. Bring to a boil, cook and stir until thick and bubbly. Cook and stir one minute more. Remove from heat and add the chopped clams and potatoes. Add salt & pepper to taste. Add one quart of half & half, stir and serve immediately with crackers. Do not boil the chowder after the cream has been added.

Chef Jamison Clark

203 Strand Street • Alexandria, Virginia
(703) 836-4442

Blackened Catfish

8 oz. Catfish fillet per person
Cajun Blackening spice
Cooking Oil

Heat about 1/4 inch of oil in a skillet. Rub the spices on each side of the catfish fillet and add to the hot oil. Cook about 4 minutes on each side or until blackened. Remove from pan and serve with black beans & rice.

Cajun Blackening Spice

Mix equal parts of Black Pepper, Paprika, Cayenne Pepper, powdered Thyme, and Oregano. Rub onto meat before pan-frying.

Black Beans & Rice

2 Cups cooked Black Beans
2 Cups cooked Rice
1 diced Red Pepper
1 diced green Pepper

1 diced Yellow Onion
3 Tsp. chopped Garlic
2 Tbsp. Butter
Salt & Pepper to Taste

Heat butter in skillet and add all vegetables and garlic. Saute 5 min. over low heat. Add beans, rice and S & P. Mix well and cook 10 min. or until hot.

Chef Jamison Clark

203 Strand Street • Alexandria, Virginia
(703) 836-4442

TAVERNA CRETEKOU

Located in Historic Old Town Alexandria, Virginia Taverna Cretekou has been a treasured eating place for 25 years. Entering through the restaurant's distinctive glass door, a transformation occurs. The traffic along King Street fades and the customer is transported to the azure seas along Greece's shores. The whitewashed walls are reminiscent of the island of Santorini, and the stone floors bring to mind the stones that pave the roads of Old Hania, Crete. The ambience is only one of the factors that transport the customer to Greece. In the tradition of long ago Ancient Greece, Taverna uses only the most wholesome ingredients in the food. Using the staple of olive oil, many wonderful dishes are created by Taverna's Executive Chef, George Maltabes.

Executive Chef George Maltabes is a native of Andros, a beautiful sun-drenched Greek island in the Mediterranean. He has over 15 years experience in numerous restaurants and hotel kitchens in Andros, New York, Florida and Greece, and is familiar with many different types of food.

 # TAVERNA CRETEKOU

818 King Street • Alexandria, Virginia
(703) 548-8688

Skewered Lamb
with Coriander Yogurt

2 Lb.lean boneless Lamb
1 large Onion, grated
5 Thyme or rosemary sprigs
Grated rind & juice of
   one Lemon
1/2 Tsp caster sugar
1/3 Cup Olive oil

Salt & pepper
Grilled Lemon wedges
For the Coriander Yogurt:
1/3 Cup natural Yogurt
1 Tbsp. fresh copped Mint
1 Tbsp. fresh chopped
   Coriander
2 Tsp. Grated Onion

To make the Coriander Yogurt, mix together the yogurt, mint, coriander and grated onion and transfer to a small serving dish.

To make the kebabs, cut the lamb into small chunks and put in a bowl. Mix together the grated onion, herbs, lemon rind & juice, sugar and oil. Then add salt & pepper and pour over the lamb. Mix the ingredients together and leave to marinate in the refrigerator for several hours or overnight.

Drain the meat and thread on to the skewers. Arrange on a grill rack and cook under a preheated for about 10 minutes until browned, turning occasionally. Transfer to a plate and garnish with rosemary sprigs. Serve with the grilled Lemon wedges and the Coriander Yogurt. Serves 4

Exec. Chef George Maltabes

TAVERNA
CRETEKOU
818 King Street • Alexandria, Virginia
(703) 548-8688

Imam Baildi

12 small baby Eggplants
about 2 lbs.
1&1/4 Cups Olive oil
Salt to taste
4 Cups sliced Onion
2 Tbsp. minced Garlic
1/2 Cup chopped Parsley

3 large Tomatoes peeled
seeded & chopped, or
2 Cups crushed tomatoes
1/2 Cup Water
1/2 Tsp. Salt
1/4 Tsp. Pepper

Preheat oven to 350°.
Cut two lenghtwise slits along each eggplant. Brush on all sides with 1/4 cup of olive oil and salt lightly. Place in a baking dish and bake for 20 minutes or until soft.
While eggplants are baking, prepare sauce:
Saute onions and garlic in remaining cup of olive oil until wilted. Add the Parsley, tomatoes, 1/2 cup of water, salt and pepper. Bring to a boil and simmer for 15 minutes. Carefully spoon some sauce into the incisions in the eggplants. Pour the remaining sauce over the eggplants and continue to bake for 10 minutes.
Serve at room temperature.

Exec. Chef George Maltabes

 **TAVERNA CRETEKOU**

818 King Street • Alexandria, Virginia
(703) 548-8688

Unusual Spaghetti Sauce

1 Lb. ground Beef
1 med. Onion chopped
4 oz. can Mushroom stems
    and pieces, undrained
2 cloves Garlic crushed
1 can Tomato Soup

1 3 oz. can Tomato paste
1 Tsp. Rosemary
1 Tsp. Thyme
1/2 Tsp. Sugar
1 Tbsp. Olive Oil
Salt & pepper to taste

Brown ground beef in olive oil. Add onion and cook until soft. Add remaining ingredients. Bring to a boil, then simmer for 1 to 3 hours. Add a little water if the sauce becomes too thick.
Serve over fresh pasta. *(freezes well)*

Chef Phil Brooks

(Chef's note: "In 1939, my aunt asked a friend in Arlington for this recipe. The friend refused to share the recipe but said she would come over and make it for my aunt, which she did. Needless to say, my aunt carefully noted what her friend stirred up! My aunt believed her friend's attitude was too silly for words and acting on that belief, she proceeded to give out the recipe for the rest of her life, with the admonition that it be shared widely. The recipe became a family favorite and I am now carrying on their work. It is a delicious spaghetti sauce.")

Philip C. Brooks
Chairman
City of Alexandria
250th Anniversary Commission

Carlyle

Grand Cafe

Carlyle Grand Cafe was named one of the top 3 restaurants in the Washington, D.C. area by the Washingtonian Magazine Reader's Poll in 1995 and 1995. Additionally, Carlyle Grand was named #2 in the top ten Virginia restaurants, and winner of the Washingtonian People's Choice Award. In 1997, Washingtonian Magazine added the Carlyle to the Reader's Favorite list in several categories: Best Restaurant, Most Underrated Restaurant, and Best Brunch. Since Chef Jackson's arrival, the Carlyle Grand Cafe has averaged annual sales of over 6.5 million and has averaged 9,000 covers per week!

Carlyle Grand Cafe

4000 South 28th Street ● Arlington, Virginia

(703) 931-0777

Carlyle
Grand Cafe

Executive Chef William A. Jackson, C.E.C.

Bill Jackson, Executive Chef of the Carlyle Grand Cafe since 1988, and managing Partner of Best Buns Bread Company, is a Certified Executive Chef and a graduate of the Culinary Institute of America(1976).

In 1995, Chef Jackson was recognized as Chef of the Year by the Washington Metropolitan Restaurant Association!

Before coming to the Carlyle Grand Cafe in 1988, Bill was Executive Chef of Pano's and Paul's in Atlanta, Georgia. While at Pano's from 1979 through 1988, the restaurant was honored with Restaurant & Institutions Magazine's Ivy Award and with Nation's Restaurant News Hall of Fame Award. Additionally, Pano's was recognized as "Best of Atlanta" by the Atlanta Magazine for six consecutive years and given a Four Star rating by the Mobil Travel Guide.

Carlyle Grand Cafe
4000 South 28th Street • Arlington, Virginia
(703) 931-0777

Lobster Cole Slaw

4 Cups Lobster meat
4 Cups Savory Cabbage
3 Cups Tomato
2 Cups White Scallions
1 Cups Chopped Chives
3 Cups Dressing

Chiffonade the savory cabbage and place in large bowl.
Add the tomatoes, scallions and chives.
Add the dressing and toss to coat.
Fold in the Lobster meat.
Pat dry the savoy leaves and lay in a mold leaving a
1 inch overhang.
Spoon Lobster-Cabbage mix into mold.
Fold cabbage leaves over and press to shape.
To serve, unmold and place on plate.
Garnish with a lobster medalion and claw.
Drizzle with Basil oil, sprinkle with a few chives
and lobster roe.

Exec. Chef William A. Jackson, C.E.C.

Carlyle
Grand Cafe

4000 South 28th Street • Arlington, Virginia
(703) 931-0777

Apple - Walnut Crostada

3 qts. Cooking Apples, peeled & cored	1 Tbsp. Sugar
	1/3 Tsp. Allspice
2 oz. Butter	1/3 Tsp. Cloves
1/2 Cup Brown Sugar	1/3 Tsp. Cinnamon

Saute apples over med-high heat with butter. Stir often so as not to burn the apples. When 1/2 cooked & slightly colored, add sugars and spices. Cook another 4-6 min. or until cooked through. Should not be all mushy. Remove from heat & cool on sheet pan, then cover and chill.

Roll out pie dough thinly and, using small bowl, cut dough to make circles. Sprinkle small chopped walnuts in center of each round and top with a scant 1/2 cup of apple filling. Bring edges of dough up and around filling by folding the edges over each other.
Brush dough with egg wash and sprinkle with small chopped walnuts and then sugar on top. Nuts should go all around the dough and not just in the center.
Let tarts chill for at least 15 minutes before baking at 350° for about 25 minutes, or until the crust is golden brown and cooked through. Let cool on pan.

Exec. Chef William A. Jackson, C.E.C.

Carlyle
Grand Cafe

4000 South 28th Street • Arlington, Virginia
(703) 931-0777

Roast Capon Breast & Maine Lobster

4 ea. Maine Lobster	1 Tsp. Thyme
8 ea. Capon Breast	3 ea. Bay leaf
2 Cups Flour	2 Tbsp. Tarragon
Salt & pepper	1 Cup Tomato
White Wine	16 pcs. ea. Carrots,
2 qts. Lobster stock	Zucchini, yellow squash
1 Cup Shallots fine chop	2 Cups Pearl Onions
1 Tbsp. Garlic fine chop	

Steam lobster and reserve broth. Lightly flour the capon and sear in moderate hot saute pan. Finish cooking in 375° oven for approx 8 to 10 minutes. Prepare the sauce. Remove capon and hold warm. Add the shallots & garlic and saute briefly. Add the tomato and white wine, bay leaf and thyme and reduce by 4/5ths. Add the stock and reduce by half. Finally, add the cream and reduce by 1/3 or desired consistency. Strain and add chopped tarragon leaves. Check for seasoning and hold for service.

Prepare the lobster: extract the claw, tail & knuckle meat. Slice tail meat into medalions. Slice capon on slight bias & reassemble alternating with lobster medalions. Splash with wine and serve immediately with the sauce.

Exec. Chef William A. Jackson, C.E.C.

Carlyle
Grand cafe

4000 South 28th Street • Arlington, Virginia
(703) 931-0777

Started in June, 1995 by Alexandria residents Balraj and Nicky Bhasin, the Bombay Curry Company is a popular neighborhood eatery in the Del Ray area. "cozy and comfortable" is how most patrons describe it. Etched glass, hanging brass temple bells and an assortment of colorful spices in bottles help to make it so. Amid the Indian fabrics, artifacts and large mirrors, there is a statue of Ganesha, the Indian god for good luck and prosperity. At the Bombay Curry Company you'll get a wonderful meal and good luck, too!

Indian cuisine lends itself to sharing, and that's the way to go says Chef/owner Balraj. Visit an Indian restaurant with friends and order different things. Along with traditional dishes, creative Chef Balraj offers many exciting entrees not found anywhere else. For a little restaurant, Bombay Curry Co. has a big heart, often represented at numerous fund-raisers around town.

Balraj Bhasin would like to show two recipes; one is a "no fail" shrimp recipe. If you have the ingredients, you are already ahead with a wonderful dinner prepared in a very short time. The other is a simple chicken curry.

3110 Mount Vernon Avenue
Alexandria, Virginia

Shrimp in Coconut Milk

1 lb shrimp, peeled deveined, tails on
1 heaped tsp fresh, finely chopped ginger
1 heaped tsp fresh, finely chopped garlic
½ tsp cayenne pepper
1 level tsp turmeric
1 level tsp cardamom powder
1/8 cup oil
2 dried hot peppers (or more)
1 heaped tsp mustard seeds
8-10 curry leaves (forget if you can't find them)
½ cup coconut milk
salt to taste
¼ cup fresh cilantro, chopped

•Put first 6 ingredients in a bowl. Mix well and leave in refrigerator   a couple of hours or until you need them.
•Heat oil in a wok and add dried whole red hot peppers (or dried chili as some call it), mustard seeds and stir around until the seeds start popping, the hot peppers turn black and the oil starts smoking.
•Add curry leaves, stir fry 10 seconds
•Add marinated shrimp. Stir fry a few minutes
•Add coconut oil and cook till shrimp are done and the milk thickens to a gravy consistancy.
Serve with white rice

Chef/owner Balraj Bhasin

Bombay Curry Company
3110 Mount Vernon Avenue
Alexandria, Virginia
(703) 836-6363

A Simple (Basic) Curry

1 lb boned chicken breast, 1 ½" cubes
¼ cup   oil
2 lg onions, evenly chopped fine
3 Tbs fresh finely chopped ginger
2 Tbs fresh finely chopped garlic
1 ½ heaped tsp coriander powder
1 heaped tsp   cumin powder
1 level tsp turmeric powder

1 level tsp gavam Masalla
(blend of Indian spices, get
from an ethnic store or borrow
a little from Bombay Curry Co.
½ cup   crushed tomatoes
¼ cup   plain yogurt
salt to taste

Heat the oil in a pan over medium heat, add evenly sliced/
chopped onions. Caramelize the onions (if the onions are not
evenly sliced, chopped, the small pieces tend to get cooked
faster, burn and blacken the curry or gravy.   It's also good
idea to keep some water/stock handy and add a few ounces to
the caramelizing onions if they start sticking to the pan
bottom, like deglazing. This process also helps to break up
the onions, resulting in a smoother sauce/gravy/curry instead
of onions and other ingredients floating around in a watery
curry). When the onions are light brown, add ginger & garlic,
saute till onions are golden brown, adding a little liquid
occasionally and stirring continuously. When browned, add
spices dissolved in an ounce or two of water. Cook a few
minutes, stirring till the mixture releases the oil and the
frying process starts again. Another minute and add tomatoes
and the yogurt. Cook until the mixture again releases oil.
Your curry is now ready but probably is not smooth, with bits
of onion and tomato. Blend and smooth in a food processor.
Return curry to pan, add chicken and ½ cup of water/stock.
Cook till chicken is done. Vary quantity of liquid to obtain
the viscosity of the gravy you personally like.
• serve with white rice
Remember there are as many ways to make this curry as there
are people, so feel free to vary seasonings to what will be right
for you.

Chef/owner Balraj Bhasin

Bombay Curry Company
3110 Mount Vernon Avenue
Alexandria, Virginia
(703) 836-6363

135

Garden Court Restaurant

at the Crystal City Sheraton

Executive Chef Leonardo Robledo was born in Guadalajara, Mexico. He learned the basics of fine cuisine from his mother, a renowned culinarian in her own right.

Chef Leonardo is a Culinary Arts graduate and has spent many years in some of the finest kitchens in this hemisphere sharpening his culinary skills. Before being selected as Executive Chef for the Sheraton here in Crystal City, he has worked for several hotel chains and resorts throughout the U.S., Mexico and the Caribbean. The Garden Court Restaurant serves a contemporary menu with a new American flair.

Chef Leonardo Robledo

Garden Court Restaurant

at the Crystal City Sheraton

Jefferson Davis Highway • Arlington, Virginia

(703) 486-1111

Seared Pineapple Relish

1 ripe Pineapple, peeled & cut in 1/2 inch slices
1 bunch Cilantro, chopped
1 small Red Pepper, diced
Juice of three Limes
Juice of two Oranges
1/2 Cup Brown Sugar
1 Tsp. crushed red Pepper
1 Tsp. Salt

On a very hot skillet or on a grill, cook the pineapple slices until dark brown, being careful not to burn them.
Dice and mix with the remainder of the above ingredients.

Crab & Jack Quesadilla
with Yellow Tomato & Black Bean Salsa

1/4 Lb. Backfin Crab meat
1/2 Lb. shredded Jack cheese
1 Tbsp. Old Bay seasoning
1 bunch sliced Scallions
4 10 inch flour Tortillas

Combine Crab meat with green onions, cheese and Old Bay seasoning. Portion the mixture on the tortillas and fold to form a half moon. Cook on a dry skillet over medium heat until cheese is completely melted. Cut into triangles and serve with Yellow Tomato and Black Bean Salsa on top.

Chef Leonardo Robledo

Garden Court Restaurant
at the Crystal City Sheraton

Jefferson Davis Highway • Arlington, Virginia
(703) 486-1111

Dishes OF INDIA

Dishes of India has become a favorite of the Hollin Hills neighborhood of Alexandria. It offers traditional elegance and décor in contemporary facilities, excellent cuisine and attentive personal service. They offer an unparalleled encounter with delectible Indian cuisine. Many visitors who have dined here have found it a surprising delight and have quickly become steady patrons.

Dishes of India's Tandoori, an egg-shaped clay oven which is charcoal-fired to extremely high temperatures, produces lamb, chicken, salmon and vegetable dishes of exotic charm and spiced superbly.

<u>Chef Ramanand Bhatt</u> has devoted over 47 years to the art of cooking and has worked in Washington, D.C. for over 16 years.

He was associated with Fine Indian cuisine in Madrid, Spain and at a hotel in India he prepared quality food for Air India, India's only international airline. He worked at Rajajee Fine Indian Cuisine in Washington and as Executive Chef at Haandi Fine Indian Cuisine in Virginia and Maryland.

In 1995 Chef Bhatt received the Chefs 2000 award from the Chefs in America Association, certifying him as one of North America's outstanding chefs.

<u>Chef Sohan Singh</u>

Sous chef Sohan Singh brings over 30 years experience to Dishes of India. He worked in Ashoka Hotel, one of India's top 5-star rated hotels. He also worked in Japan and has been in the Washington, D.C. area for 10 years.

1510-A Belleview Blvd • Alexandria, Virginia
(703) 660-6085

Murg Tikka Tandouri

Boneless breast pieces of chicken marinated in our chef's special recipe, barbecued over flaming charcoal in clay oven called "Tandoor"

4-6 pcs. boneless chicken breast
1 cup plain yogurt
2 Tbs Garam Masala*
½ Tbs white vinegar
¼ Tbs red food coloring if needed for presentation
*Garam Masala:
 5 green cardamoms
2 Tbs coriander seeds
1 Tbs cumin seeds
4 cloves
2 cinnamon sticks, in pieces
¼ Tbs black pepper
2 dried bay leaves
¼ Tbs ground mace
1 oz   fresh ginger
1 oz   fresh garlic
¼ Tbs salt

Grind all garam masala ingredients, mix with yogurt and white vinegar and marinate the chicken pieces in this sauce at least 4-6 hours prior to cooking
Skewer marinated chicken pieces and place in charcoal-clay-oven "Tandoor" at 300-400 F for at least 10-15 minutes

1510-A Belleview Blvd. • Alexandria, Virginia
(703) 660-6085

Serious Steak ☺ *Serious Seafood* ☺ *Serious Fun*

Executive Chef Paul Lombardy

Chef Paul Lombardy began his apprenticeship in 1983 and attended the Culinary Institute oa America from 1984 to 1986. In 1986 he was the Garde Manger at 40 Main St. Restaurant, a trendy 65 seat restaurant in northern New Jersey which received a Four Star rating from the New York Times. In 1987 Chef Lombardy worked at the Plainfield Country Club as the Chef Garde Manger, the year the club hosted the U.S Women's Open.

In 1988 he was the Sous Chef at Branches Restaurant in New Jersey, featuring new, and what is now called "fusion" cuisine. During his tenure, Branches was voted "Best New Restaurant" in the State of New Jersey!

Chef Lombardy was Executive Chef at Bedford's Restaurant and The Lighthouse in the resort area of the Jersey shore.In July of 1996 he joined the Sheraton team and still serves as Executive Chef at the Sheraton Suites here in Alexandria.

Fin & Hoof Bar & Grill

at the SHERATON SUITES
801 North St. Asaph Street • Alexandria, Virginia
(703) 836-4700

Grilled Shrimp with Vegetable Salsa

1 Lg. Green Pepper	1 med. Red Onion
1 Lg. Red Pepper	2 Jalapenos, seeded
1 sm. Zucchini	4 sliced Plum Tomatoes
16 Jumbo Shrimp size 10/12	1 Avocado

for the Marinade:

1 Tsp. ground Cumin	Juice of 4 Limes
1 Tsp. Chili powder	1/2 Cup Olive Oil
1 Tsp. Salt	1 Tsp. chopped Ginger
1/2 Tsp. Black pepper	1 Tsp. chopped Garlic
1/2 Cup chopped Cilantro	1 Tsp. chopped Basil
1/2 Cup Tomato juice	1 Tsp. chopped Oregano
2 Tsp. Honey	

Cut the vegetables into long strips to grill easily. Combine all marinade ingredients in blender & mix. Divide in half and marinate Shrimp & vegetables separately for 1 hour. Grill shrimp & vegetables and then chill. Dice the veggies in 3/4 inch dice. Dice 1 Avocado and marinate in same vegetable marinade.

Combine all and place salsa on a plate and arrange the Shrimp over the salsa. Garnish with Lime and fried tortilla chips.

Serves 4.

Exec.Chef Paul Lombardy

FIN & HOOF

Bar & Grill

Serious Steak ☺ Serious Seafood ☺ Serious Fun

at the SHERATON SUITES
801 North St. Asaph Street • Alexandria, Virginia
(703) 836-4700

Grilled Sirloin Steak

with Roasted Garlic Sauce & Spicy Onions

4 12 oz. Sirloin steaks	2 Bay leaves
1 oz. chopped Shallots	8 oz. Beef Stock
2 oz. whole Garlic cloves	5 oz. thin sliced Onion
1/2 Cup Red Wine	Flour

Marinate the thinly slice white onion in a good store-bought Creole spice. Coat the Garlic cloves with olive oil and salt & pepper and place in a metal pan and roast in a 400° oven until brown. Remove from oven and add the wine, shallots and bay leaf. Reduce the wine by half on the stove and then add the beef stock. Simmer to marry the flavors and lightly thicken with 1 Tsp cornstarch and 2 Tsp water, then adjust the seasoning.

Rub the Sirloin steaks with olive and salt & pepper and grill until desired doneness. Place steaks on platter to keep warm.

In a 6 to 8 in. high pan heat 3 cups vegetable oil to 350°. Remove onions from bowl and squeeze out any excess moisture, then dredge in flourseasoned with salt and cayenne pepper. Shake off excess flour and the deep-fry until golden brown and crispy. Drain on paper towels. Arrange sirloin steak on plate and top with 2 oz. of the sauce and equal amounts of the fried onions.

Exec.Chef Paul Lombardy

Grilled Shrimp & Scallops

with Spinach-Walnut Pesto over Angel Hair Pasta

8 oz. Fresh Spinach
2 oz. Parmesan Cheese
1 oz. Garlic
1 Tsp. Salt
1 Tsp. Blk Pepper
1 Cup toasted Walnuts
Juice of 2 Lemons
2&1/2 Cup Olive Oil

4 Large Plum Tomatoes
   sliced 1/4 in. thick
12 oz. Angel Hair Pasta
   cooked *al dente.*
12 U-15 Shrimp
16 Large Sea Scallops
1/2 Cup Kalamata olives,
   chopped

Combine first 8 ingredients in blender, and set aside. Toss shrimp and scallops with 2 Tsp. olive oil and 1 Ts. Lemon juice. Place sliced tomatoes on lightly oiled baking tray, season with salt & pepper and bake at 200° for about 2 to 2&1/2 hours till moisture is gone. Grill the shrimp and scallops. Toss the cooked pasta with the pesto, enough to coat and then toss in the dried tomatoes. Arrange the shrimp and scallops on top. Garnish with the Kalamata olives and some freshly grated Parmesan cheese.
Serves 4.

Exec. Chef Paul Lombardy

FIN & HOOF

Bar & Grill

Serious Steak ○ Serious Seafood ○ Serious Fun

at the **SHERATON SUITES**
801 North St. Asaph Street • Alexandria, Virginia
(703) 836-4700

Grasshopper Pie

This is a wonderful and easy summer dessert recipe, and because it's green, I am certain that it must be good for you and, of course, low fat.

Mix 1&1/2 cups chocolate wafer cookies (crushed) with 1/2 stick of melted butter and press into 8 inch glass pie plate. Refrigerate.

Melt 2/3 cup table cream with 25 full size marshmallows. Cool. Fold in 3 to 4 Tbsp. clear Creme de Cocoa, 3 to 4 Tbsp. green Creme de Menthe, and 1 cup heavy cream which has been whipped.

Pour into pie shell and refrigerate 2 hours. Eat.

Chef David Speck

David G. Speck
Councilman
City of Alexandria

101 Royal Restaurant
at the
Holiday Inn Select

Chef Ibrahim Jalloh

480 King Street • Old Town Alexandria • Virginia
(703) 549-6080

101 Royal Restaurant
at the
Holiday Inn Select

The Holiday Inn Select on King Street is one of the only hotels in the heart of the Old Town Historic Distric within walking distance of hundreds of restaurants, shops, antique stores, art galleries and historic attractions. Twice Holiday Select of the Year and Torchbearer Award winner for 1998-1999, it is home to *101 Royal Restaurant* and to *Annabelle's Garden Court Cafe.*

Executive Chef Ibrahim Jalloh

A greduate of Baltimore International Culinary College, Chef Jalloh specializes in French and Italian Cuisine and enjoys Ice Carving, pastry making and menu planning. Prior to his arrival here he was Executive Chef at Holiday Inn on the Hill in D.C., Executive Chef at Bellevue Hotel in D.C., Executive Chef at Guest Quarter Hotel in Alexandria. He was also a Catering Chef for Martin's Crosswind in Greenbelt, Maryland and Lauson Gourmet in Washington, D.C.

101 Royal Restaurant
480 King Street • Old Town Alexandria • Virginia
(703) 549-6080

Mushroom Bruschetta

1 oz. Portobello Mushrooms
1 oz. Shiitake Mushrooms
1 oz. Domestic Mushrooms
1/2 oz. Shallots
Salt & pepper to taste
2 oz. Sherry
2 oz. Butter
1 Tsp. fresh Thyme
2 oz. Olive Oil
Italian Bread

Cut bread into slices on the bias.
Brush slices with butter and grill.
Slice all mushrooms.
Heat Olive oil in saute pan.
Add mushrooms and shallots and saute.
Add Thyme.
De-glaze with Sherry and reduce.
Add in butter.
Season to taste with salt & pepper.
Cover toasted bread slices with the mixture.
Heat and serve.

Chef Ibrahim Jalloh

101 Royal Restaurant
at the Holiday Inn Select

480 King Street • Old Town Alexandria • Virginia
(703) 549-6080

Chicken Wrap

1 Boneless Chicken breast
1 Onion
2 Peppers
1 Tsp. Fajita seasoning
1 Tsp. Chili Powder
4 oz. Butter
1 Tsp. Cumin
2 oz. Garlic

Pesto Tortillas
2 oz. Sour Cream
2 oz. Salsa
2 oz. Guacamole
3 oz. Mixed greens
Tortilla chips
Dressing

Grill the chicken and the vegetables. Cool and julienne.
Heat a large skillet and add the butter.
Add the garlic, onions, chicken and peppers.
Add the spices.
Cook 10 minutes and remove from heat.
Spread each pesto tortilla with guacamole.
Top with 3 oz. of the chicken mixture.
Roll up tortilla and cut in half.
Place greens on plate and then the chicken wraps.
Add dressing for the greens.
Garnish with chips and condiments on the side.

Chef Ibrahim Jalloh

101 Royal Restaurant
at the Holiday Inn Select

480 King Street • Old Town Alexandria • Virginia
(703) 549-6080

Heart-Healthy Salmon

8 oz. Fresh Salmon
pinch of Thyme
1/2 oz. Garlic
1 Lemon
3 oz. Vegetables
Salt & Pepper to taste

Combine the juice of the Lemon with the
garlic and Thyme.
Marinate the Salmon in the mixture.
Place the marinated salmon in a steamer
along with seasonal vegetables and potato
and spices.
Steam for 10 to 15 minutes.
Arrange on plate with some greens and
garnish.
Healthy & delicious !

Chef Ibrahim Jalloh

101 Royal Restaurant
at the Holiday Inn Select

480 King Street • Old Town Alexandria • Virginia
(703) 549-6080

THE ATHENAEUM

The Athenaeum is owned and maintained by members of
the Northern Virginia Fine Arts Association.
It is the site for presentations of a stimulating mix
of the fine arts offered to the public, either for free or
at very low fees.
It was the first branch of the Virginia Museum of Fine Arts.
Built in 1851 as a bank, it is an excellent example of
Greek Revival architecture.
All are invited to become members.

201 Prince Street • Alexandria, Virginia

Kotta Pilafi

Greek Chicken with Rice

3 whole Chicken breasts, split, skin removed
   (boneless or bone-in)
1 Tsp. Olive Oil
1 #2&1/2 cam whole Tomatoes
1 medium Onion, chopped
2 Cups Water
2 Chicken Bouillon cubes
1 Tsp. Cinnamon
Salt & pepper to taste
1 Cup Long Grain Rice

Saute chicken in oil until golden brown, using low heat. Add everything else except rice. Cover and simmer for 15 minutes. Add rice and stir to mix evenly. Cover and simmer for 20 minutes until rice is cooked, adding more water as needed. Serve chicken and rice with a bowl of cold, low-fat sour cream to be spooned over the hot rice. Can be cooked a day ahead as it gets even tastier when the flavors mingle.
Good accompanied by a green salad, and zucchini flavored with oregano and garlic, and a lemon-flavored dessert.
Makes six servings.

Chef Mary Gaissert Jackson

Mrs. Jackson is Executive Director of Northern Virginia Fine Arts Association
at
THE ATHENAEUM

Happy Cooking - Chef

La Bergerie

Located in the Heart of Historic Old Town,
La Bergerie consistently offers the finest in
French cuisine and Basque specialties in a
relaxed and charming setting.
Always voted one of the area's favorite restaurant, La Bergerie welcomes new diners and
faithful regulars with genuine warmth and
friendliness.
La Bergerie is decorated with French countryside paintings and Crystal chandeliers. Its charming and intimate atmosphere provides the
perfect ambiance for any special occasion.

Chef Jean Campagne-Irbacq is a member of the
Academy Culinaire de France, Association des
Maitre Cuiciniers de France and Commanderie
de Cordons Bleus de France. He has been given the
Ordre de Merit Agricole, as well as silver stars by
the French government for his culinary efforts.

Washingtonian Magazine rates La Bergerie as one
of the very finest restaurants in the entire
Washington, D.C. metropolitan area !

218 North Lee Street • Alexandria, Virginia
(703) 683-1007

Fax (703) 519-6114   www.LaBergerie.com

Sea Scallops Navarraise

32 Sea Scallops	2 Whole Red Peppers
1&1/2 Lb. fresh Fettucine	2 Whole Green Peppers
1/2 Cup Orange Concentrate	2 oz. Butter
1/2 Cup Olive Oil	Salt and Pepper
2 Tbsp. white wine Vinegar	2 oz. Bayonne ham finely cubed

Roast red and green peppers for 5 minutes. Peel and slice peppers into julienne strips.

For the Sauce: In a blender, combine the olive oil, orange concentrate, vinegar and a pinch of salt & pepper. Blend for 15 seconds. Reserve in small container.

Cook Fettucine al dente.
Melt Butter in large hot pan. Lightly flour Scallops and sear until golden on both sides.
Finish cooking in oven for 5 or 6 minutes. Keep warm.

Toss Fettucine with julienne of peppers and Ham and salt and pepper.
Place tossed pasta in center of serving tray, pour Orange Sauce around the Pasta and arrange scallops on Sauce.
Serves 4
(optional: Broccoli fleurettes for presentation)

Chef Jean Campagne-Ibarcq

218 North Lee Street • Alexandria, Virginia
(703) 683-1007

Veal Normande

1&1/2 Lb. Veal Loin cut into 2 oz. Scaloppini	2 oz. Heavy Cream
2 oz. Butter	1 Cup sliced Mushrooms
3 Shallots peeled & chopped	1 Cup Beef or chicken Broth
	1 oz. Calvados

Lightly flatten the veal scaloppini, then pat each with salt, pepper and flour.

Over medium heat, put 2 oz. butter in a skillet and when hot, cook the veal on both sides, 3 to 4 minutes on each side.

Place veal on serving tray and keep warm.

Remove the fat from the skillet and add Shallots, the sliced mushrooms and cook over medium heat until done.

Add the Calvados. Let reduce by half, add the Heavy Cream and let reduce. Add the broth and let simmer for 4 to 5 minutes. Season to taste and pour over the veal.

Serves 4.

Chef Jean Campagne-Ibarcq

218 North Lee Street • Alexandria, Virginia
(703) 683-1007

Fax (703) 519-6114   www.LaBergerie.com

Tarte Au Citron

(Lemon Tart)

1 Tart Shell - precooked
4 Lemons
8 Eggs
12 oz. Whipping Cream
12 oz. Sugar
1 Egg for eggwash

Wash lemons and grate the zest. Squeeze the juice out and set aside with the zest.

Combine the 8 eggs and sugar in mixing bowl and whisk until well blended. In second bowl, whisk the cream until it just starts to thicken. Pour over the egg mixture, add the lemon juice and zest. Mix all together lightly for about 10 seconds.

Brush the inside of the precooked tart shell with the eggwash and bake in 300° oven for 3 minutes.

Pour the filling into the tart shell and bake for 1 and 1/2 hours. When cooked, the lemon tart should be kept at room temperature.

Bon Appetit !

Chef Jean Campagne-Ibarcq

218 North Lee Street • Alexandria, Virginia
(703) 683-1007

Alexandria Archaeology Museum

Alexandria Archaeology is the City of Alexandria's community archaeology program, and a division of the Office of Historic Alexandria. City archaeologists, volunteers and students work with citizens and developers to locate sites important to our community's past and when necessary, excavate them scientifically. The artifacts in the Alexandria Archaeology Collection, from more than 150 sites, span over 10,000 years of human history. Together with historic records, photographs, maps and oral histories, the artifacts are a valuable community resource. Alexandria Archaeology seeks to preserve and study these tangible remains of our heritage for public enrichment and enjoyment.

Come visit the Alexandria Archaeology Museum and laboratory and see archaeology in action! Exhibits, hands-on learning activities, study collections and publications all help bring archaeology above ground. Satisfy your curiosity about the past through archaeological discovery.

Alexandria Archaeology Museum
a division of the
Office of Historic Alexandria
located in
Torpedo Factory Art Center
105 North Union Street
Alexandria, Virginia

Pumpkin Bread

4 Eggs beaten
3 Cups Sugar
1 Cup Salad Oil
2/3 Cup Water
2 Cups Pumpkin (1 can)
3 Cups Flour
1 Tsp. Baking Soda
1/2 Tsp. Salt
1 Tsp. Cinnamon
1 Tsp. Nutmeg
2/3 Cup chopped Nuts

Mix ingredients 1 thru 5 in the order given.
Then mix the dry ingredients sifted together.
Pour batter into well greased loaf pan, 2/3's full.
Bake for 1 hour at 350°.
Makes 3 loaves.

Chef Jean Federico

Jean Taylor Federico
Director
Office of Historic Alexandria

SIAM 815
THAI RESTAURANT & PUB

Authentic Thai food in Historic Old Town Alexandria. Whether chilli-hot and spicy or comparatively bland, harmony is the guiding principle behind each dish at Siam 815. The cuisine is a marriage of centuries-old Eastern and Western influences harmoniously combined into something uniquely Thai. With Buddhist backround, Thais shun use of large animals in big chunks. Big cuts of meat are shredded and laced with herbs and spices. Traditional Thai meals are served all at once, permitting diners to enjoy a combination of different dishes and tastes. Thai food is normally eaten with a fork and spoon. All meats are served in tender bite-sized slices or chunks, eliminating the need for a knife.

A harmonious blend of the spicy, the subtle, the sweet and the sour, equally satisfying to the eye, nose and the palate,

Delicious authentic Thai cuisine served in a delightful atmosphere in the heart of Old Town Alexandria at very reasonable prices!

815 King Street • Alexandria, Virginia
(703) 519-7399

Khao Pad

(Fried Rice)

3 Tbsp. Peanut Oil
7 oz. Boneless skinned
  Chicken breast
1 Tbsp. Chopped Garlic
1 Med. Onion, sliced
2 Eggs

4 Cups Cooked Rice
1 Tomato cut into 8 wedges
1 Chopped Spring Onion
2 Tsp. Fish Sauce
1 Tsp. Sugar
1 Tsp. White Pepper

Cut Chicken breasts lengthwise into 1/2 inch thick slices.
Heat the Peanut Oil in a Wok or pan and add the Chicken pieces and Garlic and mix well over the heat for 1 minute. Then add the onion and cook for another minute. Break in the eggs and mix very well.
Stir in the already cooked Rice and the rest of the ingredients.
Stir well and continue cooking for another 2 minutes and then serve immediately with Cucumber slices and whole Spring Onions.

SIAM 815
THAI RESTAURANT & PUB

815 King Street • Alexandria, Virginia
(703) 519-7399

Phat Thai

3 Cups Narrow Rice
    Noodles
1/2 Cup sliced Chicken
    meat in small strips
4 Shrimp
2 Eggs
1/3 Cup Soy bean curd
    cutin small slivers
1 Cup cooking Oil
1 Tsp. chopped Garlic
1 Tsp. chopped Shallot
    or onion

1 Tsp. ground dry Red Chili
4 Tbsp. Sugar
4 Tbsp. Fish Sauce
4 Tbsp. Vinegar
1/2 Cup Bean sprouts
1/3 Cup Scallions
    chopped to 1 inch
1 Lime for garnish
1/4 Cup sliced Carrot
2 Tbsp. ground roasted Peanuts

Fry the Garlic and onion until turned yellow. Add the
Chicken and fry until cooked. Pour in the Shrimp, Soy
bean curd and break eggs into the pan and scramble.
Add Sugar, Fish sauce, Vinegar, ground Chili and stir well.
Pour in the noodles and mix well. Add the Spring Onions
and about 3/4's of the bean sprouts. Stir fry until cooked.
Spoon onto heated platter and garnish with ground roasted
Peanuts, the rest of the bean sprouts, Carrot slices,
and sliced Lime.

SIAM 815
THAI RESTAURANT & PUB

815 King Street • Alexandria, Virginia
(703) 519-7399

Tom Kha Kai
(Chicken Coconut Soup)

2 Cups Coconut Milk	5 Tbsp. Fish Sauce
6 thin slices young Galangal	2 Tbsp. Sugar
2 Stalks Lemon Grass	1/2 Cup Lime Juice
lower portion cut into	1 Tsp. Black Chili Paste
1 inch and crushed	1/4 Cup Cilantro
5 fresh Kaffir leaves torn	5 Green Thai Chili peppers
in half	crushed
8 oz. sliced chicken breast	

Combine half the coconut milk with the galangal, Lemon grass and Lime leaves in a large saucepan and heat to boiling.
Add the Chicken pieces, Fish Sauce and Sugar.
Simmer for about 4 minutes or until the Chicken is cooked.
Add the remaining coconut milk and heat just to boiling.
Place the Lime juice and Chili Paste in a heated serving bowl and pour the soup over.
Garnish with Cilantro leaves and crushed chili peppers.

SIAM 815
THAI RESTAURANT & PUB

815 King Street • Alexandria, Virginia
(703) 519-7399

Chicken Satay

1&1/2 Lbs. Boneless Chicken
1/4 Tsp. roasted Coriander
   seed powder
1/4 Tsp. roasted Cumin seed
   powder
1/4 Tsp. Black Pepper
1/4 Tsp. Tumeric powder
1/4 Tsp. Curry powder
3 slices Galangal

1/2 Tbsp. Lemon Grass
   finely chopped
1 Tbsp. Salt
5 cloves diced Garlic
1 Cup Coconut Milk
2 Tbsp. Vegetable Oil
2 Tbsp. Sugar
Small wooden skewers

Slice the Chicken breast finely, lengthwise about 1 to 1&1/2".
In a blender, mix together the Coriander seed, Cumin seeds,
Pepper, Tumeric, Curry powder, Galangal, Lemon Grass,
Salt and Garlic. Pour the blended ingredients into the
Coconut Milk. Add the Sugar and Vegetable Oil an blend
again so that all the ingredients are well blended.
Add the Chicken slices and marinate for 2 hours.
Thread the chicken onto the skewers. Pour the marinade
into a pot and heat until boiling. Place the skewered chicken
on a charcoal grill and apply the sauce to the Chicken while
turning over. When cooked, serve with a satay sauce and a
cucumber sauce.

SIAM 815
THAI RESTAURANT & PUB

815 King Street • Alexandria, Virginia
(703) 519-7399

Seaport Center

Built in 1998, the Alexandria Seaport Foundation Seaport Center is a floating post and beam, cedar decked, two story museum nestled among the City Docks in the heart of Old Town Alexandria.

Within the Seaport Center you will find a maritime environmental sciences laboratory, an extensive maritime history library, a wooden boat-building school and small boats on the water.

On board our dory *Potomac* - the only floating classroom based in Northern Virginia - students learn marine science, maritime history, the mathematics of navigation and the physics of sailing. The *Potomac* also doubles as a pleasure boat for members, their guests and visitors to Alexandria's historic waterfront.

ALEXANDRIA·SEAPORT·FOUNDATION

Alexandria Seaport Foundation
Cameron Street at the Potomac River
(703) 549-7078

www.capaccess.org/asf

Joe Theismann's
RESTAURANT

Like Joe, the former Redskin quarterback, Joe Theismann's Restaurant is unique in character. Altho it may look like a "Jock Bar" on big game days, Joe's mostly is a comfortable friendly place to meet for a good time and a great meal. The varied menu offers multi-course gourmet cuisine to simple sandwiches: homemade pastas, fresh seafood, awesome steaks, salads, burgers. Enjoy outside dining on the patio or reserve the roof for a cocktail reception. A great neighborhood corner gathering place since 1986!

Chef Louis Aguirre

Chef Louis came to the United States in 1986 from his home country of El Salvador. He joined Joe Theismann's in 1989 as a dishwasher. He was rapidly promoted, acquiring a new language and culinary skills at lightning speed. He became Assistant Chef, training under Chef Anna Maria DeGennaro. To further hone his talents, he moonlighted as Assistant Chef under Bill Jackson of the Carlyle Grand Cafe. As now Head Chef at Joe's, he combines his experience to create menu items and daily specials that utilize seasonally fresh ingredients and contemporary food trends.

Joe Theismann's
RESTAURANT
1800 Diagonal Road • Alexandria, Virginia
703-739-0777

Tropical Shrimp

& Gingered Pineapple

Saute 16/20 sized shelled & deveined shrimp in oil
with salt & pepper.
Add finely chopped onion & garlic.
Add fresh orange juice, Lime juice, minced scallions
and chopped cilantro.
Garnish with gingered pineapple & whole cilantro.

Gingered Pineapple

1 Pineapple, quartered lengthwise
2 Tbsp. fresh Lime juice
1&1/2 Tbsp. minced Ginger
1 Tbsp. Sesame Oil
1/2 Tsp. Salt
1/4 Tsp. Pepper

Marinate pineapple in mixture of above ingredients
for 30 minutes and then grill.

Chef Louis Aguirre

Joe Theismann's

RESTAURANT

1800 Diagonal Road • Alexandria, Virginia
703-739-0777

Balsamic Vinaigrette

Joe Theismann's House Dressing

1/2 Cup Tamari
1 Cup balsamic Vinegar
3/4 Cup Water
1/4 Cup Dijon Mustard
1&3/4 Cup Ex Virgin Olive oil
2 Cups blended oil
2 Tsp. minced Garlic
4 Tsp. fresh Thyme

Chef Louis Aguirre

RESTAURANT

1800 Diagonal Road • Alexandria, Virginia
703-739-0777

Carrot Cake
with Cream Cheese Frosting

2 Cups Flour	1&1/2 Cups mazola oil
2 Tsp. Baking Powder	4 Eggs
1&1/2 Tsp. Baking Soda	2 Cups grated Carrots
1 Tsp. Salt	1 8&1/2 oz. can crushed
2 Tsp. Cinnamon	Pineapple (drained)
2 Cups Sugar	1/2 Cup chopped Walnuts

Sift the dry ingredients (flour, baking powder, soda, salt and cinnamon) and mix together. Add the sugar, oil and eggs. Mix well. Add the carrots, pineapple and nuts. Grease and flour three 9 inch pans. Bake 35 to 40 minutes at 350°.

Cream Cheese Filling:

1/2 Cup Butter	1 Tsp. Vanilla extract
8 oz. Cream Cheese	1 Lb. Confectioner's Sugar

Soften butter and cream cheese - but not too soft. Blend all ingredients. To thicken, add more confectioner's sugar.

Chef "Del" Pepper

**Redella S. Pepper
Councilwoman
City of Alexandria**

Christ Church
Alexandria, Virginia
1773

Christ Church

The Rev. Pierce W. Klemmt, Rector
118 North Washington Street
Alexandria, Virginia

Visitors Welcome Daily 9am to 4pm, Sundays 2pm to 4:30pm

Christic Church

Construction on this mid-eighteenth century Georgian-style church commenced in 1767 under James Parsons and was completed in 1773 by John Carlyle.

George Washington worshiped here and, his pew is preserved in its original configuration. Robert E. Lee married Washington's step-great granddaughter, Mary Custis, and attended Christ Church throughout his life when in the area. He was confirmed here, together with two of his daughters on July 17, 1853. A silver plaque on the chancel rail marks the spot.

In the twentieth century Christ Church has honored its heritage and preserved its colonial structure while continuing to minister to its parishioners and the community. It is a tradition for the President of the United States to visit this church some time during his administration. Here on January 1, 1942, President Franklin Roosevelt and British Prime Minister Winston Churchill came for a World Day of Prayer for Peace during World War II.

Historic Christ Church is maintained solely by the parishioners and by donations.

Christ Church

The Rev. Pierce W. Klemmt, Rector
118 North Washington Street
Alexandria, Virginia

Visitors Welcome Daily 9am to 4pm, Sundays 2pm to 4:30pm

Geranio

For 22 years Geranio, on famous King Street in Old Town, has combined excellent service with simply prepared and precisely executed cuisine, which is based in modern Italian, with influences from French and American cooking. Here fall and winter selections center on hot, rich dishes that comfort and sooth, while spring and summer focus on colorful seafood and salads that refresh and restore. The dishes are created combining color, texture and flavor.

Fine dining in a lovely setting has made Geranio a favorite of Alexandrians and visitors for a long time.

<u>Chef/Owner/Manager Troy Clayton</u> began his restaurant career washing dishes, as do so many of the great chefs. He learned his craft thoroughly as apprentice to Master Chef Donaldo Soviero at La Scula Di Cucina in the Umbrian of Italy, and has since gained experience at "Le Bristol" in Paris and "190 Queen's Gate Restaurant and Bistrot" in London, along with many well known restaurants in Washington, D.C,, among them the"Palladin" in the Watergate Hotel. In 1996, Troy co-founded the now famous Steak Around, Inc and served as Vice President of Operations for this multi-unit franchise. In 1998 he became owner of Geranio Ristorante, an Alexandrian landmark.

<u>Chef Jeffrey Galkin</u> has a B.S. in Political Science from Radford University and an A.S. in Culinary Arts from Johnson and Wales University. He has been a chef at the Greenbrier Country Club, "Chez Francis" in Cap Ferrat, France, Washington's "La Colline". Now at Geranio, Chef Galkin is responsible for the daily operations and has played a vital role in taking Geranio into the limelight of regional cuisine.

722 King Street • Alexandria, Virginia
(703) 548-0088

Country Tomato Bisque

4 slices white country Bread
1 Tbsp. Red Wine Vinegar
1 Tbsp. Sugar
4 cloves Garlic finely chopped
3 oz. Ex Virgin Olive Oil
1&1/2 Lbs. Plum Tomatoes liquidized
1 Can 15 oz. Tomato Juice
1 bunch spring Onions trimmed
1 Cucumber peeled & seeded
2 Red Peppers, roasted, peeled & seeded
2 Tbsp. fresh Basil chopped
Salt & pepper to taste

Liquidize the country Bread, Vinegar, garlic
and sugar together.
Slowly add the oil followed by the rest of the
ingredients.
Puree until smooth.
Season to taste.
Serve well chilled.

RISTORANTE
Geranio

722 King Street • Alexandria, Virginia
(703) 548-0088

Saffron Risotto

1 small Onion, chopped
1 piece bone marrow
7 Tbsp. Butter
1 qt. Vegetable (or chicken) Stock
1/2 Cup White Wine
1&1/3 Cup Arborio Rice
1/2 Tsp. Saffron soaked in warm stock
1/4 Cup grated Parmesan
Salt & pepper to taste

Bring the stock to a boil in a deep pot. Saute the onion and rice in a large pan. Add the wine and allow to cook into the rice, stirring constantly. Add the saffron and begin to ladle in the stock slowly, allowing each ladle to be absorbed before adding the next. When the rice is 3/4 cooked, but still nutty, allow the rice to thicken to a consistancy that will just hold on the plate. Add the parmesan cheese and marrow and butter to your taste. Check the seasoning and allow to rest 2 minutes.
Serve hot.

RISTORANTE
Geranio

722 King Street • Alexandria, Virginia
(703) 548-0088

Osso Buco

6 oz. Ex Virgin olive oil
6 Veal shanks with marrow
1 Tbsp. Garlic finely diced
1 Tbsp. Carrot finely diced
1 Tbsp. Onion finely diced
1 Tbsp. Celery finely diced
1 Cup Flour
1 Tbsp. Pancetta or smoked bacon
1/3 Tsp. Thyme
1/2 Cup Tomato paste
1&1/2 Cup White Wine
6 Cups Veal stock
Salt & pepper to taste
chopped Parsley

Heat oil, add the vegetables, garlic and pancetta, saute gently. Dust the shanks in seasoned Flour and, in a separate pan, brown the shanks in oil. Deglaze the pan with white wine and a bit of stock. Add the tomato paste to the vegetables and continue cooking 10 minutes without allowing the paste to stick to the pan. Add the shanks and liquor to the vegetables and stir. Add the diced garlic and bring to a boil and set to braise in a 300° oven covered, until tender.
Serve with a bit of the sauce(may need reducing) and Parsley. This dish is perfect with Saffron Risotto.

RISTORANTE

Geranio

722 King Street • Alexandria, Virginia
(703) 548-0088

Flourless Chocolate Cake

18 oz. Chocolate
2 Tsp. Vanilla
3 Tbsp. espresso
3 Tbsp. Brandy
18 Tbsp. Butter

1&1/2 Cups Sugar
1&1/2 Cups ground almonds
1&1/2 Cups Double Cream
9 Egg Yolks
9 Egg Whites

Melt the chocolate with the coffee, brandy, vanilla
and butter. (do not mix while melting)
Whisk the yolks with the sugar until pale and ribboned
and then add the ground almonds. Fold these two
mixes together. Fold in the cream whisked firm,
followed by the whites which have been whisked to
stiff peaks.

Using a 9 inch springform pan, bake in a 300° oven
for 40 minutes or until beginning to set.....or cook
in a bain marie for 1&1/2 hours.

Chill the cake and then warm the pan slightly
when ready to remove the cake.
Serve at room temperature with whipped cream
and fresh strawberries.

RISTORANTE

Geranio

722 King Street • Alexandria, Virginia
(703) 548-0088

Apple, Armagnac & Prune Beggars Purse

10 Apples(Granny Smith, peeled, cored
      and sliced thin)
1/4 Tsp. Ground Cloves
1/4 Tsp. Ground Cinnamon
1 Lemon - juice of
1/2 Cup Armagnac
8 oz. unsalted butter, melted
8 oz. Prunes, pitted & chopped
20 sheets Filo
6 Tbsp. Sugar
2 Tbsp. orange water

Marinate the apples in lemon juice, armagnac and spices the day before required.

Mix the orange water, 2 Tbsp. marinade and butter. Cook the apples in this mixture on very high heat for 3 to 5 minutes. Add the prunes and allow to cool.

Using 1/2 sheet filo cut into a square, butter and sugar 6 sheets, layering each one on top of the previous diagonaly. Place your pastry in a shallow blinis pan and fill with apples. Drizzle with marinade and fold the ends up to form a "beggars purse". Bake in a 400° convection oven until golden and serve with creme fraiche.

RISTORANTE

Geranio

722 King Street • Alexandria, Virginia
(703) 548-0088

The Pita House was opened in 1992 by the Tarek Moukalled family after immigrating from Lebanon. They offer the first and only source of Lebanese cuisine in Old Town. The location at 407 Cameron Street is in the heart of Old Town Alexandria.

Chef Tarek Moukalled was born and raised in Beirut, Lebanon and inherited his mother's love of fine cuisine as well as many of her wonderful recipes.

In addition to many fine Lebanese vegetarian dishes such as Hommos, Falafel, Fool, Tabouleh and Baba Ghanouj, the Chef also offers fine main courses like Chicken Kababs and Lamb Kakabs.

407 Cameron Street • Alexandria, Virginia
(703) 684-9194

Hommos

1 Garlic clove
3 oz. Lemon juice
3&1/3 Lbs. Chick Peas(dry
    Mexican peas, <u>not</u> canned)
3/4 Tsp. Salt
2 oz. Sesame Paste
3 oz. of the Chick Pea broth
1/4 Tbsp. Baking Soda

Soak the chick peas in water with the baking soda over-night. Boil the chick peas for approximately 45 minutes, or until soft. Srain the peas and reserve the liquid. Place the peas in a blender, add garlic, salt, sesame paste and 3 oz. of the reserved chick pea broth. Blend until chick peas are fine and creamy. Add the lemon juice and blend for 5 minutes. Empty Hommos from blender and refrigerate. Before eating, splash olive oil on top and some Paprika for decoration. Serve cold with Pita bread for dipping. Serves 5

Chef Tarek Moukalled

The Pita HOUSE

407 Cameron Street • Alexandria, Virginia
(703) 684-9194

Fool

2&1/2 Garlic cloves
1 Tsp. Salt
1 Lb. Fava Beans
1&1/4 oz. Lemon juice
1/4 Tsp. Cumin powder
1 oz. Chick peas
1/4 Tsp. Baking soda

Soak Fava beans and chick peas separately in water with baking soda overnight. Boil Fava beans and chick peas separately for about 45 minutes or until soft. (the Fava beans will take longer to soften).
In a deep round pot, mash the garlic with the salt and add the fava beans and chick peas and mash halfway with the garlic & salt. Add lemon juice and Cumin and blend.
Serve warm with a splash of olive oil on top. If desired, sprinkle Parsley and tomato on top and garnish with side of pickles, olives, onions and dry mint.
Serve with Pita bread.
Serves 5

Chef Tarek Moukalled

The Pita HOUSE

407 Cameron Street • Alexandria, Virginia
(703) 684-9194

Ramsay House

Located at 221 King Street in the heart of Old Town Alexandria, the Ramsay House is a cultural icon, generally referred to as the oldest house in the city, dating to 1751 or earlier. It was originally the home of William Ramsay, one of the founding trustees of Alexandria and a prosperous merchant.

Ramsay House is currently the home of the City's Visitor Center and offices for the Alexandria Convention & Visitors Association.

The Alexandria Convention & Visitors Association (ACVA) is a public-private membership organization whose mission is to market Alexandria the city as a travel destination for both leisure and business travel. Marketing initiatives include advertising and media coverage, industry trade shows, meeting closely with meeting planners and tour operators. The ACVA hosts *www.FunSide.com*, an informative and interactive web site, publishes an annual *Official Visitors Guide to Alexandria*, and sponsors the FunSide Forum, northern Virginia's only community-wide marketing forum for tourism.

Ramsay House
221 King Street

ALEXANDRIA
THE FUN SIDE OF THE POTOMAC

THE FUN SIDE OF THE POTOMAC

Alexandria Convention & Visitors Association, Inc.

Anni's Fun Side Chicken

4 deboned Chicken breasts	1 Egg
3/4 Cup crumbled Feta	1/2 Cup Water
6 slicesdried Beef fine chopped	1/2 Cup Butter
2 Tbsp. fine chop Cilantro	1/2 Tsp Garlic powder
1/4 Cup fine chop Walnuts	1/2 Tsp. Oregano
1 Cup fine Bread Crumbs	1 Green Onion

Make "stuffing" by mixing crumbled Feta cheese, cilantro, dried beef and walnuts. Slice chicken breasts along the side deeply enough to make a pocket. Fill pocket with stuffing. Once stuffed, the seam should meet at the edge.

Mix egg and water. Mix bread crumbs, oregano and garlic. Dip each breast in egg wash and then into bread coating. Place in a glass baking dish on a raised rack. Melt the butter and finely slice the green onion. Make a line down the center of the chicken breast with the green onion. Baste each breast with the melted butter. Repeat the basting two times during the baking time. Bake in preheated 350° oven for 1 hour.

Serve with Rice Pilaf and green beans.

Chef Anni Clinger

THE FUN SIDE OF THE POTOMAC

Alexandria Convention & Visitors Association, Inc.
221 King Street ● Alexandria, Virginia
703-838-4200   800-388-9119
ACVA@funside.com

IL PORTO

The original owner of the building which is now Il Porto Ristorante was a retired sea captain. He constructed the building like his ship - sturdy and sound in wall and beam. He stocked it with silks from the far east, silver from Spain, jewels from England and France and - to his misfortune - a valued family heirloom of one of his customers. The unhappy customer has the captain arrested and tried in the town square. As a result of the captain's quick demise, the building had a new owner, Madame LeCleaque, who turned it into a house - not a home! Business was brisk until a pesky customer shot the Madame and her girls fled into the night. The building remained empty for years.

After the Civil War, two southern ladies opened a shop to sell family treasures. When they retired, a wine press and distillery were found in the basement. Perhaps the family recipe sold better than the antiques! The building became a butcher shop with meat selling for 5¢ a pound. A German artist used the building during World War II as a studio, specializing in paintings of the Torpedo Factory.

The Roaring Twenties saw a speakeasy here, then during the 40's, a Nazi family moved in and set up a radio network disguised as a fix-it shop. Now, restored to its natural charm, the old building is now the home of great Northern Italian cuisine.

121 King Street • Old Town Alexandria, Va.
(703) 836-8833

Pollo Veneziana

1 Lb. sliced boneless
    Chicken Breast
1 Broccoli floret chopped
2 Roma Tomatoes diced
6 Basil leaves chopped
1 clove Garlic minced
1/2 Tsp. Salt(to taste)
1/2 Tsp. Pepper(to taste)
2&1/2 Tbsp. Olive Oil
1 Cup Chicken Broth
1 Cup White wine(Chablis)
1/2 Lb. Penne pasta
1/2 Lb. Fusilli pasta

Cook pasta as directed on package.
Saute the chicken in olive and garlic.
Add wine and chicken broth and bring to a boil.
Add Basil, salt, pepper, broccoli and tomatoes.
Reduce heat and simmer until chicken is thoroughly cooked.
Add cooked pasta, toss and serve.
Serves about 4

Executive Chef Carlos Campos

IL PORTO
121 King Street
Old Town Alexandria, Va.
(703) 836-8833

Executive Klaus Keckeisen

Tuscany's Executive Chef Klaus Keckeisen was born in Germany and apprenticed at a small hotel in Lake Constance. From there he moved to a resort hotel in Sanberg, Switzerland. A brief stint in Ireland at the Hill of the Fairies Ardnaside was followed by work in a gourmet restaurant on Paradise Island in the Bahamas. From ther he was hired as Banquet Sous Chef at the prestigious Flagship JW Marriott in Washington, D.C.. He was quickly promoted to Executive Sous Chef and then was made Executive Chef at the Crystal Gateway Marriott. He recently has been promoted to Executive Chef at the Crystal City Marriott, where he in now responsible for the operations of both Marriott hotels. Tuscany's was recently voted as "Best Hotel Restaurant" in Arlington County and specializes in Northern Italian Cuisine.

in the Crystal Gateway Marriott Hotel
1700 Jefferson Davis Highway • Arlington, Virginia
(703) 920-3230

Scampi All' Aglio

5 Shrimp, size 16/20
1 oz. Olive Oil
1 oz. White Wine
1 oz. Fresh Lemon Juice
1 Tsp. Garlic
6 oz. Capers
1 oz. Butter

Heat saute pan until almost smoking.
Saute olive oil.
Add shrimp, sear and turn over.
Add garlic.
De-glaze pan with white wine.
Add Lemon juice and Capers.
Reduce and then whisk in the butter.
Remove shrimp and fan on warmed plate.
Pour sauce over the shrimp.
Garnish with chives.
Serve as appetizer.

Executive Chef Klaus Keckeisen

Capellini con Pollo Griglia

4 oz. Grilled Chicken	1 oz. Olive Oil
2 oz. Proscuitto	6 oz. double Cream
1 oz. sun-dried Tomatoes blanched	5 oz. Capellini
	Salt & pepper to taste
1 oz. Basil chiffonade	2 oz. fresh Parmesan
1 Tsp. chopped Garlic	1 Tsp Roma Concasse
1 Tsp. chopped Shallots	1 sprig opal Basil

Thin slice (julienne) the grilled chicken.
Julienne the proscuitto.
Saute the shallots and Garlic in olive oil.
Add the chicken, proscuitto and sun-dried tomatoes.
De-glaze with the White Wine and herbs.
Reduce and add cream and 1 oz. of freshly grated
Parmesan cheese.
Cook the Capellini pasta al dente.
Place pasta in center of heated large plate.
Top with the cream sauce.
Garnish with 1 oz. of freshly grated Parmesan and
Roma concasse.
Top with sprig of Basil and serve.

Executive Chef Klaus Keckeisen

in the Crystal Gateway Marriott Hotel
1700 Jefferson Davis Highway • Arlington, Virginia
(703) 920-3230

Spinach all' Aglio

4 zo. Blanched Spinach
1 oz. Olive Oil
1 Tsp. chopped Garlic
1 oz. Roasted Pepper
pinch of salt & pepper
1 oz. Grilled Eggplant

Heat olive oil in saute pan.
Add the garlic and saute.
Add vegetables and saute briefly for a few minutes.
Salt & pepper to taste.
Serve as side dish.

Executive Chef Klaus Keckeisen

in the Crystal Gateway Marriott Hotel
1700 Jefferson Davis Highway • Arlington, Virginia
(703) 920-3230

THE WAREHOUSE
BAR & GRILL

12/11/99

Chef Sert Ruamthong has worked at The Warehouse Bar
& Grill for almost ten years. Originally from Thailand,
Sert is a graduate of the Siam Technical College and has
trained at the prestigious Culinary Institute of America
in Hyde Park, New York.

Before joining the Warehouse in 1990, Sert honed his skills
working alongside Executive Chef Michael Fouctuer at
the Radison Hotel in Alexandria. Chef Fouctuer, a native of Paris, exposed Sert to the nuances of fine French
cuisine which complimented his already extensive knowledge of Oriental and Asian food preparation. Since arriving in Old Town, Sert has expanded his French-Asian
background to include American Creole and Cajun dishes
which are the backbone of the Warehouse menu. Sert uses
a wide range of fresh seasonal products available here such
as Soft Shell Crabs, Shad Roe, fresh Florida Rock shrimp,
Chesapeake Bay Rockfish on his daily specials. Also try
one of his signature desserts like "Hezelnut Creme Brulee"
or "Triple Chocolate Decadence".

214 King Street • Alexandria, Virginia
(703) 683-6868

Grilled Veal Chop
with Wild Mushrooms

4 Veal Chops (Frenched Rib Chops)
Olive Oil for brushing
Cajun spices
3 Tbsp. unsalted Butter
1 Lb. assorted Mushrooms, chopped

1/4 Cup chopped Tasso Ham
1 Tbsp. Veal demi-glace
1/2 Cup White wine
1 Cup Heavy Cream
Salt & Pepper to taste
chopped Fresh Parsley

Brush veal chops with olive oil and dust with Cajun spices. Grill over high heat until cooked to desired doneness. Set aside and keep warm while making sauce.

To a preheated saute pan, add butter and mushrooms - saute over high heat until mushrooms start to release their juices.

Add tasso ham and veal demi-glace and reduce the liquid. De-glaze the pan with white wine and add the cream. Add salt and pepper to taste and the reduce to proper consistency.

Arrange cooked veal chops on each serving plate, drape on the sauce and top with fresh chopped Parsley
Serves 4

Chef Sert Ruamthong

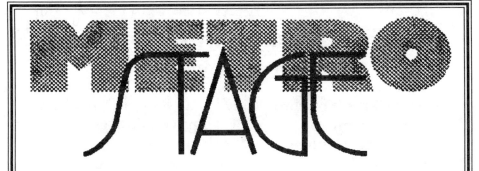

As the oldest professional theatre in Northern Virginia, MetroStage is dedicated to plays by established and emerging playwrights which are chosen for their social, political, literary, and entertainment value. It also offers a children's theatre series, cabarets, and FirstStage, a series of staged readings presented as part of the theatre's commitment to the development of new work.

MetroStage presents challenging contemporary American plays and musicals and is also recognized for its South African dramas and British comedies. MetroStage's work speaks to the concerns and passions of our time by showcasing the dynamic writing and performances of the best local and regional artists.

1201 North Royal Street
Alexandria, Virginia
(703) 548-9044

Pecan Tassies

A great dessert for a buffet table after a press opening at the theatre.

Mix:
1 Cup Butter
6 oz. cream Cheese
2 Cups Flour
Divide pastry dough into 4 parts, forming 12 balls from each part and pressing with thumb into mini-muffin tins.

Cream:
1/2 Cup Butter
1 Cup Sugar
Add:
1 Egg beaten
1&1/2 Cups chopped Pecans
1 Cup chopped Dates
1 Tbsp. Vanilla
Fill the uncooked pastry cups and bake at 350° for 30 to 40 minutes. Cool on racks before removing.

Chef Carolyn Griffin

Carolyn Griffin
Producing Artistic Director

1201 North Royal Street
Alexandria, Virginia
(703) 548-9044

Carlyle House

When the Scottish merchant John Carlyle built his riverfront home in 1752, it was the grandest mansion in the new town of Alexandria. Carlyle House gained its place in history when British General Edward Braddock used it for his headquarters in 1755. It was here that Braddock summoned five colonial governors to what John Carlyle called"...the Grandest Congress...ever know on this Continent...", a council held to discuss the strategy and funding for the French and Indian War.

With its stone construction and manor-house design, the Carlyle House was unique to Alexandria. It's design was believed to have been inspired by an engraving of Craigiehall, an elaborate Scottish country house illustrated in Vitruvius Scoticus, a popular architectural patternbook of the time. The elegance of the stone cornice which graces the façade, a rare feature in colonial Virginia, is matched by the superbly carved woodwork of the former parlor.

121 North Fairfax Street • Alexandria, Virginia

Carlyle House

Originally, the Carlyle House stood on and acre lot overlooking the Potomac River, but as the shoreline was filled in, other buildings were erected around it. In 1801, John Carlyle's son-in-law, William Herbert, constructed the bank building which today still stands on the corner of the property. In the mid-19th century, Carlyle House became part of a hotel complex owned by a local furniture manufacturer. Following his tenure the house began a period of slow decline. In 1970 the Northern Virginia Regional Park Authority purchased the dilapidated and restored it to its former glory. It was opened to the public as part of a Bicentennial celebration. One of the most popular features of the house is the unplastered room that illustrates, layer by layer, the construction and restoration history of the structure.

Business and social ties made John Carlyle a leading citizen of the Northern Neck. His marriage to Sarah Fairfax allied his with one of the most prestigious and powerful families in the colony. His partnership in two merchant firms and his business acumen brought him outstanding wealth for those times. His numerous appointments to public office brought him recognition.

Each December the Carlyle House prepares for the coming Christmas season. Christmas Day was a holy day, not a holiday in the eighteenth century. However, the twelve nights after Christmas leading to Twelfth Night were a time of socializing with friends and family. Gifts were exchanged on January 6. The following recipe is one that we make every year for the Carlyle House Christmas table. It is an eighteenth century recipe. "King Cakes"

¾ cup butter	1 ¼ cups flour
¾ cup sugar	1 teaspoon mace
2 egg yolks	½ cup currants
1 Tablespoon cream	

Beat the butter and sugar together until mix is light and fluffy. Combine egg yolks and cream, then stir in flour and mace and currants. Spoon the batter in small dollops onto 2 buttered baking sheets. Bake in 375-degree oven 12 to 15 minutes. Makes about 30 cakes.

121 North Fairfax Street • Alexandria, Virginia
(703) 549-2997

Lee-Fendall House Museum

Revolutionary War hero General "Light Horse Harry" Lee, the father of Robert E. Lee, sold the lot at the corner of Oronoco Street to Alexandrian lawyer, Philip Fendall, who built this wood frame house in 1785. In the 1790s Philip married Mary Lee, the sister of "Light Horse Harry". George Washington, a close personal friend of Fendall and Lee, dined here nine times according to his Mt Vernon journals. Here also "Light Horse Harry" wrote the Farewell Speech from Alexandrians to George Washington upon his departure to be inaugurated as first President of the United States. Generations of the famous Lee family continued to live in the house until 1903.

Now restored to its early Victorian elegance, the House is interpreted as a Lee family home of the 1850-1870 period and is furnished mostly with pieces donated by descendants of the Lee family.

The Lee-Fendall collection of antique dolls represents the range of 19th century technologies in dollmaking. A permanent exhibit of 19th and 20th century dolls' houses reflect in miniature America's architecture, decorative arts and domestic life.

The Lee-Fendall House is listed on the National Register of Historic Places.
Visiting Hours: Tues.- Sat. 10am - 4pm
Sunday 1pm - 4pm

614 Oronoco Street • Alexandria, Virginia

Lee-Fendall House Museum

Turkey Soup
A Lee Family Recipe

20 lb. Turkey carcass
1 lb. Country ham (scraps will do) or bacon
3 qts. Water
2-3 .Medium onions, roughly chopped
1-2 .Carrots, roughly chopped
1-2 ribs Celery, roughly chopped
½ cup Parsley, chopped
1 cup Ham liquor, if available
2 cups Half and half
1-2 Tbs. Flour, if desired as thickening

Break up carcass. Cover with water. Add ham
broth, if used. Add onions and carrots and simmer
at least 1 ½ hours. Add celery, simmer about 1
hour more. Strain off broth. Discard vegetables.
Pull lean ham and turkey to shreds and reserve.
Discard bones. If broth is not intensely flavored,
cook down. Before serving, return turkey and ham
to broth and add half and half. If thickening with
flour, stir in cold water to make a paste and stir
into soup. Simmer, stirring occasionally, for at
least 20 minutes. Correct seasonings. Put chopped
parsley in bottom of tureen or bowls and pour soup
over.
Serves 10-12

614 Oronoco Street • Alexandria, Virginia

Fudge Cake

4 oz. Baking Chocolate
2 sticks Butter or oleo
4 Eggs
2 Cups Sugar
1 Cup sifted Flour
1 Tsp. Vanilla
Powdered Sugar

1) In a sauce pan, melt together the baking chocolate and butter. Let the mixture cool.

2) Beat the eggs well. While beating, sift in the sugar.

3) Add 1/2 the melted chocolate to the eggs.

4) While beating slowly, add the sifted flour.

5) Add the remaining melted mixture and vanilla.

6) Pour mixture into a pan lined with wax paper. Bake at 350° for 15 to 20 minutes, careful not to overcook.

7) Once cooled, invert and sprinkle with powdered sugar.

Chef Jim Gilmore

**Commonwealth of Virginia
Governor James Gilmore**

POTOMAC RIVERBOAT COMPANY

- Cherry Blossom

- Admiral Tilp

- Matthew Hayes

- Miss Christin

205 The Strand • Alexandria, Virginia
(703) 684-0580

Grilled Shrimp
with Dijon Vinaigrette

3 Lb. large Shrimp 21/25's
Olive Oil
2 Or 3 cloves Garlic crushed
1/4 Cup Wine Vinegar
1 Tbsp. Sesame Oil
2 Tbsp. fresh Basil
Salt & pepper to taste
Sauce for shrimp

Peel & devein shrimp. Marinate in mixture above overnite if possible. Heat gas grill or charcoal until Hot. Thread shrimp on bamboo skewers for easy turning. Grill shrimp 2 to 3 minutes on each side brushing with marinade until done.

Sauce for Shrimp:

2 cloves Garlic crushed   1/4 Cup Vinegar
3 to 4 Tbsp. Dijon Mustard

In a bowl, combine all ingredients. Mix well. Add olive oil a little at a time, whisking constantly. Salt & pepper to taste. Serve as dip for shrimp.

Chef Michelle Brogger - Panache

Potomac Riverboat Company
205 The Strand • Alexandria, Virginia
(703) 684-0580

Doorways to Old Virginia

Twilight or night time tours are a combination of history, legends and folklore bringing to life exciting events of the old seaport town of Alexandria.

Stories are wound around unusual historical facts concerning everyday life, the death of George Washington, his townhouse in Alexandria, the boyhood home of Robert E. Lee, Christ Church, where both men were members, and a tavern and 18th century ballroom where George dined and danced his last dance at his own Birthday Ball in February 1799.

Other stories are told at the Tomb of the UnKnown Soldier of the Revolutionary War and at the mass grave of 34 Confederate soldiers.

Guests follow a lantern-carrying colonial-attired guide, passing Georgian and Federal style buildings that are separated by dark secluded cobblestone alleyways.

The tour ends in a graveyard where you may step on someone that you are just dying to meet.

Tour begin at
The Ramsey House
King & Fairfax Sts.

CREEP

through the DARKEST NIGHT
following pale LANTERN light

Don't miss Alexandria's ORIGINAL GHOST &
GRAVEYARD TOUR through the haunted streets
of historic Old Town!

Martha Washington's Ginger Cakes

3/4 Cup Soft Butter	4 Cups sifted Flour
3/4 Cup Lard or margarine	2 Tsp. Baking Soda
2&3/4 Cups White Sugar	2 Tsp. each: Cinnamom,
2 Eggs	Cloves, Ginger
1/2 Cup dark Molasses	

Cream shortening until soft and light. Slowly cream in 2 cups of the sugar. Beat in the eggs and molasses. Sift in all dry ingredients until well mixed. Dough will be soft. To help in handling, chill briefly. Roll pieces of dough into 1 inch balls, then roll each ball in remaining sugar. Place on well-greased baking sheet about 3 inches apart to allow for spreading.

Bake at 375° for 12 to 15 minutes. Cool slightly and lift with a spatula to a wire cooling rack. These will soften in very hot weather.

Yields about 100

Doorways to Old Virginia

CREEP
through the DARKEST NIGHT
following pale LANTERN light

Don't miss Alexandria's ORIGINAL GHOST & GRAVEYARD TOUR through the haunted streets of historic Old Town!

Chief's Special
Pepper Spray Chili

1&1/2 Lb. Ground Beef
1/2 Lb. ground Country Sausage
1/4 Lb. Kielbasa cut in small pieces
1 chopped Green Pepper
1 chopped Onion
1 Garlic clove minced
1 28oz. can whole peeled Tomatoes, undrained

1 28oz. can crushed Tomatoes
2 16oz. cans red Kidney beans
1 Tbsp. Chili powder
1 Tsp. ground Cumin
1/2 Tsp. Salt (to taste)
2 Tbsp. Brown Sugar
1/2 Tsp. Cayenne Pepper(this is the same ingredient used in police pepper spray, but please don't try the cop's version)

Saute the meats, onion, green pepper and garlic in a large heavy skillet until well browned, stirring to crumble the beef and sausage. Drain off the excess grease and stir in remaining ingredients. Smash tomatoes with the back of a wooden spoon, cover and simmer for 1 to 1&1/2 hours.

Chef Charles Samarra

Charles E. Samarra
Chief of Police
City of Alexandria

Fort Ward Museum & Historic Site

Fort Ward Museum inter-prets the site's history and features exhibits on a variety of Civil War topics. Patterned after a Union Headquarters, the Museum houses a broad collection of Civil War artifacts, including objects related to Alexandria's Civil War past.

Armed with 36 guns mounted in 5 bastions, the Fort was a model of 19th century military design and engineering. Fort Ward was named for Commander James Harmon Ward, the first Union navel officer to be killed in the war.

Fort Ward Punch

1 can 5-Alive Citrus concentrate
2 liter ginger ale

Make a frozen ring of cherries, sliced oranges, sliced lemons and sliced limes and pour citrus and ginger ale over. Garnish with more of the fruit

**Fort Ward Museum & Historic Site
4301 West Braddock Road
Alexandria, Virginia
*(703) 838-4848***

Janet's Chicken Soup

One 4 to 5 Lb. Chicken
Salt & pepper to taste
Several sprigs of fresh Parsley or Dill
1 small Onion
5 - 6 Carrots sliced
5 - 6 Celery stalks sliced
1 Qt. boiling water per Lb. of Chicken
1 Chicken Bouillon cube

Boil the water and add chicken and other ingredients.
Continue cooking on a medium flame for about 2 hours.
Skim before serving and enjoy.

Chef Janet Barnett

Janet Barnett
Deputy Director
Recreation, Parks & Cultural Activities
City of Alexandria

The Women's History Walk Project

A Legacy Gift from the Commission for Women, in partnership with Alexandria Archaeology, in Celebration of Alexandria's 250th Anniversary

The site of the City of Alexandria is largely on property once owned by Margaret Brent, considered the nation's first woman lawyer and the first woman who demanded the right to vote. From these strong roots came many women who have contributed much to our community, from the 17th century to the present.

We began this project in 1998 and have quickly come to realize that the Women's History Walk effort will be the work of many years. As we continue our research, we invite everyone with any valuable information found in their homes, attics or memories to share with us what is known for inclusion in the "walks" that are developed.

City of Alexandria, Virginia

Commission for Women

110 N. Royal Street, Room 201

Alexandria, Virginia

ALEXANDRIA
VIRGINIA
1749 **250** 1999
YEARS

CITY OF ALEXANDRIA
VIRGINIA

Spicy Seafood Stew

3/4 Lb. Large Shrimp peeled,
and deveined
1/2 Lb. Rockfish cut in chunks
1 doz. Mussels, scrubbed
1/4 Cup Butter
1/4 Cup Flour
1 clove Garlic minced

1/4 Cup grated Swiss cheese
1 16oz. Can whole Tomatoes
2 fresh Tomatoes, chopped
1/4 Cup chopped red Pepper
1/4 Cup chopped green Pepper
1 Tbsp. chopped green chilies

Chop 1/3 of the shrimp into quarters; keep the remainder whole for adding to the stew later. In a large, heavy saucepan, melt the butter over low heat, and blend in the flour. Add the cream and garlic and stir over low-moderate heat until the mixture thickens. Add the grated cheese, stirring constantly until the cheese melts. Add the chopped shrimp, canned tomatoes, fresh tomatoes, peppers and chilies. Add salt & pepper to taste. Simmer the stew on low-moderate heat for 20 minutes, stirring occasionally; do not allow to boil. If it becomes too thick, add a little milk and stir to blend. In the last 15 minutes of cooking, add the remaining shrimp and rockfish. In a separate saucepan, slowly steam the mussels until they open; discard any that do not open. Add the mussels to the stew as you ladle it into bowls.
Serves 4. Nice with crunchy fresh bread and a green salad.

(Like the women of Alexandria, this stew reflects a range of ingredients of all flavors, sizes, shapes and colors - and has just the right amount of spice to make things interesting! The seafood base reflects Alexandria's role as a port city and our proximity to the bounty of Chesapeake Bay.)

City of Alexandria, Virginia
Commission for Women
110 N. Royal Street, Room 201
Alexandria, Virginia

ALEXANDRIA
VIRGINIA
1749 **250** 1999
YEARS

Alexandria Black History Resource Center
638 North Alfred Street • Alexandria, Virginia

The Alexandria Black History Research Center is located in the Parker-Gray district of the city. Constructed in 1940 as the Robinson Library, it was the African American community's first public library. With desegregation in the 1960s, the building was converted to use for community service programs. In 1987, the City Council placed the operation of the center under the direction of the Office of Historic Alexandria. Here can be found paintings, photographs, books and other memorabilia documenting the African American experience in Alexandria and Virginia from 1749 to the present.

Next door, The Watson Reading Room is a research repository focusing on issues of African American history and culture.

The Black History Resource Center provides ongoing lectures and tours.

Alexandria African American Heritage Park
Duke Street on Holland Lane
Dawn to Dusk

The Alexandria African American Heritage Park includes a 19th African American cemetery. It preserves interesting and varied plant life and sustains a wetland area that provides a home for mallards, painted turtles, beavers and crayfish in their natural habitat. The memorial sculptures are the creation of sculptor Jerome Meadows. The focal point of the park is a sculpture group of bronze trees called "Truths that Rise from the Roots Remembered".

Little Maids Tea Punch

(that truly packs a Punch)

To three cups of strong green tea, put the rind of 6 lemons sliced very thin, 1&1/2 Lbs. fine sugar and juice of 6 lemons. Stir together & strain. Add 1 qt. of good rum. Fill glasses with crushed ice when used. The mixture will keep bottled. If this is too thick for your liking, add sparkling water to thin. Should serve 8 to 10; however it depends on the company you keep. The Little Maids use this punch regularly at all their gatherings and never dilute it.

Little Maids Best Pound Cake

Cream together 1 Lb. creamy butter and 1 Lb. fine sugar. Add the well beaten yolks of 12 eggs. Stiffly whip the remaining whites. Sift 1 Lb. of Flour. Then add the egg whites and flour alternately to this mixture. Beat lightly and then pour into a well greased and floured mold pan. Bake in a moderate oven, 375° for approximately 1 hour. Check regularly with a broom straw for doneness. The Little Maids always serve this specialty with their finest Lemon curd.

The Little Maids of History

Bonnie Fairbank
(703) 751-8887

Pat Sowers
(703) 960-5751

The Little Maids of History

Living History Performers

Bonnie Fairbank and Pat Sowers are Performing Artists in the Washington area who have appeared in a broad range of roles depicting historical personages either authentic or hypothetical. These roles include all classes of society from the common colonial tavern wenches, well-heeled gentry ladies of refinement, Regency ladies, Civil War heroines, Victorian apothecary apprentices, 1920's Dolls, to 1945 canteen entertainers. They specialize in promoting colonial history programs for K - 12 and were the creators of the first History Camp in Alexandria.

Wearing reproduction clothing using first person interpretation, the Little Maids present programs to meet the needs of the client or site. They can also provide a mini-museum of antique items of the period for hands-on activities.

Bonnie Fairbank
(703) 751-8887

Pat Sowers
(703) 960-5751

The Blue Point Grill has been awarded 3 stars and a blue ribbon by Washingtonian Magazine. It features fresh seafood and a raw bar with farm raised oysters. And there is free underground parking!

Chef Andre J. Hopkins

Chef Andre J. Hopkins' philosophy is to obtain simplicity in cooking and elegance in taste. Having grown up on the southern cooking of North Carolina, he has developed a distinctive love of and respect for food. His goal is to have the customers leave relishing the goodness of the food.

BLUE POINT GRILL
600 Franklin Street
Alexandria, Virginia
(703) 739-0404

Seared Pink Peppercorn and Coriander
Crusted Yellowfin Tuna

6 - 7 oz. Yellowfin Tuna
loin cuts
1 Tbsp. Coriander seed
3 Tbsp. Pink Peppercorns

1 Tsp. Black Peppercorns
1/4 Tsp. Kosher Salt
1/3 Cup Sutton Place Extra
Virgin Olive Oil

1) Combine coriander, peppercorns and salt. Coarsely grind in a pepper grinder.

2) Set aside 6 Tbsp. of the olive oil. Pour 1 Tbsp. over each Tuna loin cut, turning to coat both sides.

3) Generously sprinkle ground pepper mixture over both sides of fish.

4) Add enough oil to coat bottom of pan. Heat on high but not to smoking, approximately 2 minutes. Adjust flame to medium high.

5) Place coated tuna in pan, sear both sides to desired doneness.(This tuna is best rare to medium-rare. The exact time will depend on the thickness of the slice. You will be able to judge by the appearance on the side of the tuna.)

Serve with Roasted Eggplant-Pomegranate Ragout.

Chef Andre Hopkins

200 Franklin Street
Alexandria, Virginia
(703) 739-0404

Roasted Eggplant-Pomegranate Ragout

1 Large Eggplant peeled & cubed
1/2 Cup Extra Virgin Olive oil
1 small Red Onion chopped
4 cloves Garlic, minced
1 Cup V-8 Juice

1/2 Cup Pomegranate juice
(concentrated)
1/4 Tsp. Cayenne pepper
1/4 Cup Black olives cut in 1/2
1/4 Cup fresh chopped Mint

1) Toss eggplant in olive oil(reserve 2 oz.) and roast for 15 minutes in 350° oven.

2) Heat remaining oil in 1 qt. saucepot until hot. Cook onion until slightly softened, add garlic and ginger. Cook 2 minutes.

3) Using spatula, add roasted eggplant to saucepot. Stir to combine and cook for 5 minutes.

4) Add remaining ingredients(except mint), salt & pepper to taste. Stir, ensuring no items are stuck to the bottom of pot. Bring mixture just to a boil; reduce heat and simmer until thickened, about 10 minutes, stirring often to avoid sticking.

5) Remove from heat and stir in the mint. Adjust seasoning as needed. Keep warm for service.

Chef Andre Hopkins

200 Franklin Street
Alexandria, Virginia
(703) 739-0404

Hawaiin Mahi

1 each Mahi-Mahi fillet 8 oz.
1/4 Cup Macadamia nuts crushed
Olive Oil
2 oz. dry White Wine
4 oz. Pineapple juice
2 Tbsp. Butter, softened
Salt & fresh ground pepper to taste

Heat olive oil in saute pan over medium heat, but not smoking.
Combine breadcrumbs and crushed macadamia nuts. Completely coat each fillet and sear in heated oil flesh side first, until lightly browned. About 3 minutes per side.
Add white wine and pineapple juice. Simmer for 3 minutes then cover and simmer for 5 minutes. Add butter and swirl in the pan to make a sauce. Season with salt and pepper to taste.

Suggested accompaniments:
Citrus Rice or Wasabi mashed potatoes and a colorful mixture of vegetables.

Chef Andre Hopkins

200 Franklin Street
Alexandria, Virginia
(703) 739-0404

Poached Salmon

Cooking ? I love to cook for other people - I suppose I like the social part of cooking rather than the food part of cooking.

At Thanksgiving we invite around 30 "orphans" to our "ranch" in Fauquier County, Virginia. Everyone who comes brings food to share and we always have more than we could ever eat. We cook the Turkey and a poached salmon. I actually own a 3 foot salmon poacher. The salmon is purchased to fir the poacher and feed a lot of people. You would think that we would learn exactly how to cook the salmon, but every year it is a bit different. We fill the area below the rack with white wine, capers, and garlic cloves. Then we pour a fish broth over the salmon and sit the fish on the rack and spread the poacher over two burners on the stove. After nearly an hour it is done. We then put the salmon on a platter. We cut up thin slices of cucumber and make "fish scales" and surround the fish with lemon and olives.

Chef Lois Walker

Lois L. Walker
Councilwoman
City of Alexandria

Old Town Black-eyed Pea Soup

1&1/2 Lbs. Dried Black-Eyed Peas
4 Strips Bacon, coarsely chopped
4 Links Breakfast Sausage, chopped
2 Ribs Celery, chopped
1 Med. Onion, chopped
1 Large Carrot, chopped

1 Med. Red Pepper, chopped
1 Med. Green Pepper, chopped
3 Cloves Garlic, chopped
2&1/2 Tbsp. Cumin
1&1/2 Quarts Chicken Stock
2 Bay Leaves

Soak Peas in cold water overnight. Drain & discard water. Brown Bacon and Sausage in pot, then add Celery, Onion, Carrot & Peppers, Garlic and Cumin. Cook til vegetables are tender.

Add Peas, Chicken Stock and Bay Leaves. Partially cover and simmer gently for approximately 1 hour, adding more water or stock if needed.

Add Salt & Pepper to taste. Let cool a bit. Then Puree all or part as desired for texture.

Serve in heated bowls with a dollop of Sour Cream if desired.

Makes about 10 one-cup servings.

The **Virginia Company**

Alexandria • Charlottesville
Norfolk • Richmond

104 South Union Street
Alexandria, Virginia
(703) 836-3160

INDEX - *HISTORIC SITES*

INDEX - RESTAURANTS

INDEX - *RESTAURANTS*

INDEX - *"Celebrity" Chefs*

Recipe
Index

Grilled Shrimp w/ Vegetable Salsa	141
Grilled Veal Chop - Warehouse Bar & Grill	189
Gumbo Spice Mix	19
Hawaiin Mahi - Blue Point Grill	212
Heart-Healthy Salmon - 101 Royal	149
Herb crusted Rainbow Trout - Stella's	85
Hoisin Sauce - Portner's	60
Hommos - Pita House	177
I Got the Blues Salad - Azalea	118
Imam Baildi - Taverna Cretekou	126
Irish Meggies - Murphy's	94
Irish Potato Cake - Murphy's	93
Irish Potatoes - Murphy's	94
Irish Soda Bread - Murphy's	95
Jambalaya Griddle Cakes	16
Janet's Chicken Soup - Janet Barnett	203
Jumbo Lump Crab Cakes	75
Khao Pad - Siam 815	159
Kiki Alitcha - Demera	105
King Cakes - Carlyle House	193
Kotta Pilafi - Mary Jackson	151
Lega Tibs - Demera	105
Linguine with Wild Mushrooms - ECCO	48
Lobster Cole Slaw - Carlyle Grand Cafe	130
Macaroni & Cheese	31
Mahogany Sauce	18
Maine Mussel Chowder - Clyde's	89
Mango Chipotle Ketchup	82
Mexican Chocolate Brownie - Santa Fe East	99

Seafood Stew, Union Street — 14
Seared Pineapple Relish - Garden Court — 137
Shepherd's Pie - Irelands Own — 72
Shiitake Mushroom & Cabbage Consomme — 117
Shrimp & Scallops Grilled - Fin & Hoof — 143
Shrimp in Coconut Milk - Bombay Curry . — 134
Skewered Lamb w/ Coriander Yogurt — 125
Skillet Roasted Lemon Chicken — 45
Sour Cream Chocolate Cake - Vola Lawson — 101
Sour Cream Pound Cake - Patsy Ticer — 113
Spicy Rosemary Tuna - Portner's — 57
Spicy Seafood Stew - Women's History Proj. — 205
Spinach all Aglio - Tuscany's — 187
Stuffed Trout - Seaport Inn — 51
Taragon Cream Sauce - ECCO — 47
Tarte au Citron - La Bergerie — 155
Tea Punch - Little Maids — 207
Tibs - Demera — 104
Tom Kha Kai - Siam 815 — 161
Tortellini ala Boscaiola — 33
Tropical Shrimp - Joe Theismann's — 165
Turkey Soup - Lee family — 195
Union Street Gumbo Base — 19
Unusual Spaghetti Sauce - Phil Brooks — 127
Veal Monte Carlo - Cedar Knoll Inn — 111
Veal Normande - La Bergerie — 154
Whole Grilled Rockfish - Stardust — 116